CROCHET
FROM BEGINNERS TO ADVANCED

2 BOOKS IN 1

THE COMPLETE STEP BY STEP GUIDE TO LEARN CROCHETING IN A QUICK AND EASY WAY CREATING YOUR FAVORITE PATTERNS IN COMPLETE AUTONOMY

PATTY WILSON

© **Copyright 2021 - Patty Wilson - All rights reserved**

This document is geared towards providing exact and reliable information in regard to the topic and issue covered.

From a Declaration of Principles which was accepted and approved equally by a Committee of the American Bar Association and a Committee of Publishers and Associations.

In no way is it legal to reproduce, duplicate, or transmit any part of this document in either electronic means or in printed format. All rights reserved. The information provided herein is stated to be truthful and consistent, in that any liability, in terms of inattention or otherwise, by any usage or abuse of any policies, processes, or directions contained within is the solitary and utter responsibility of the recipient reader. Under no circumstances will any legal responsibility or blame be held against the publisher for any reparation, damages, or monetary loss due to the information herein, either directly or indirectly.

Respective authors own all copyrights not held by the publisher. The information herein is offered for informational purposes solely and is universal as so. The presentation of the information is without contract or any type of guarantee assurance.

The trademarks that are used are without any consent, and the publication of the trademark is without permission or backing by the trademark owner. All trademarks and brands within this book are for clarifying purposes only and are owned by the owners themselves, not affiliated with this document.

Table of Contents

BOOK 1 : CROCHET FOR BEGINNERS

Introduction 15

Chapter 1: Crochet Basics (Tools, How to hold hook, and Yarn) 17

- Hook.. 17
- Yarns... 24
- Tapestry Needle 29
- Scissors 31
- Stitch Markers 33
- Crochet Book 34
- Darning Needle 34
- Tape measure 35
- Hook Organizer 36
- Yarn Bowl 37
- Row Counters 37
- Blocking Mat 38

Chapter 2: How to Read and Understand Crochet 39

- Level of Difficulty 39
- Practice 39
- Materials 40
- Reading Stitch Pattern Abbreviations 40
- Crochet Terminology 44
- Reading Diagrams 46
- Check the Gauge 50
- Counting Stitches 52
- Instructions and symbols 53

5

Chapter 3: Basic Stitches 57
    MAKING A SLIP KNOT 57
    SINGLE CROCHET (SC) 59
    HALF TREBLE STITCH 60
    TURNING CHAIN 64
    DOUBLE CROCHET STITCH 65
    HALF DOUBLE CROCHET (HDC) 68
    CHAIN STITCH 69
    TREBLE CROCHET 71
    DOUBLE TREBLE CROCHET (DTR) 73

Chapter 4: Beginner Patterns and Projects 75
    SIMPLE AS PIE WINTER SCARF 76
    SCRAMBLED EGG WASHCLOTH 78
    CUTE WHITE FLOWER 79
    GOLDEN DAISY 80
    COLOR BLOCK BAG CROCHET PATTERN 81
    HIGHLAND RIDGE PILLOW FREE CROCHET 84
    AFRICAN FLOWER HEXAGON 86
    COOLEST HEADBAND EVER 89
    GRANNY SQUARE 90
    BABY SQUARE 94
    CHIC SOAP POUCH 96
    CROCHET POTHOLDER 98
    FALL CROCHET BUNTING 105
    CROSS BODY BAG LOVE 108
    TUBE PENCIL CASE 111

Chapter 5: How to Crochet For Right-Handers & Left-Handers
.... 115
    RIGHT HANDED 115

LEFT HANDED 119
WHAT IS THE DIFFERENCE BETWEEN RIGHT & LEFT-HANDED CRAFTERS?
.... 127

Chapter 6: Animal Crochet 129
BUMBLEBEE 129
PENGUIN 132
BABY DRAGON 145
LAMB 156

Conclusion 167

BOOK 2 : CROCHET FOR BEGINNERS-ADVANCED GUIDE

Introduction 171
Chapter 1: Advanced Stitches 173
PICOT STITCH 173
MOSS STITCH 175
TEXTURED CROCHET STITCH 176
CHECKERBOARD STITCH 177
POPCORN STITCH 180
V-STITCHES 181
PUFF STITCH 181
CABLE STITCH 183
CLUSTER STITCH 186
BASKETWEAVE STITCH 187
MOSS STITCH 190
SEED STITCH 191
SHELL STITCH 194
SURFACE SLIP STITCH 195

7

Chapter 2: Crochet for both English and American 197

AMERICAN OR UK / INTERNATIONAL CROCHET TERMINOLOGY 197
HERE ARE SOME SUGGESTIONS AND STRATEGIES FOR DECIDING 199
THE DIFFERENCE BETWEEN AMERICAN AND BRITISH CROCHET TERMS 201
CROCHET ABBREVIATIONS 202
HOW TO READ STITCH PATTERNS FOR BOTH ENGLISH AND AMERICAN? 203
LIGHTWEIGHT TEXTURED STITCH PATTERNS 212

Chapter 3: Techniques 217

JOINING YARNS 217
INCREASE/DECREASE 219
FASTENING OFF 222
WEAVING IN TAILS SECURELY 223
CHANGING COLORS 223
SEWING TOGETHER 227
SEWING ON BUTTONS 227
OVERLAY CROCHET 228
LACE CROCHET TECHNIQUES 231
MAKING POM POMS 249
CROCHET WITH PLASTIC RINGS 252
CROCHET FLOWERS 253
BUTTONHOLES 254
MAKING RIDGES 256
SHELL BORDERS 258
WORKING A SQUARE 259
EDGINGS 260
WORKING IN ROWS 264
BLOCKING YOUR CROCHET 266
BLOCKING METHODS 268
WORKING IN THE ROUND 270
WORKING IN A SPIRAL 276

BACKSTITCH SEAM JOINING 277
HOW TO WORK A FRONT POST 279
HOW TO WORK A BACK POST 281

Chapter 4: Tunisian Crochet 283
TOOLS 283
CONSTRUCTION 284
FABRICS 284
GETTING STARTED 285
THE FOUNDATIONAL ROW AND THE FORWARD PASS 286
KNIT STITCHES AND THE FORWARD PASS 290
KNIT STITCHES AND THE REVERSE PASS 291
FINISHING OR BINDING 292
BASIC TUNISIAN CROCHET STITCHES 293

Chapter 5: Animal Crochet 301
BUTTERFLY 301
BUMBLEBEE 311
SEAMUS SHAMROCK 314

Chapter 6: Advanced Patterns and Projects 321
SUPER SCARF CROCHET PATTERN 321
EASY TEXTURED SCARF 323
EASY CROCHET COFFEE COZY 325
ROPE/CLOTHESLINE EASY CROCHET BASKET 327
MARKET BAG 329
LEG WARMERS 332
BLANKET SCARF 333
CROCHET FACE SCRUBBIES 334
DAINTY BABY SWEATER 336
QUICK LITTLE CROCHET BAG 339

Modern Taupe Crochet Belt 341
Crochet Flower Bracelet 343
Hand Towels 345
Simple Crochet Wrap Bracelet 348
Two Color Bracelet 350
Striped Circle Coasters with a Scalloped Edge 352

Conclusion 355

BOOK 1 : CROCHET FOR BEGINNERS

LEARN HOW TO CROCHET IN A QUICK AND EASY WAY WITH STEP BY STEP PATTERNS AND ILLUSTRATIONS TO CREATE YOUR FAVORITE PROJECTS IN COMPLETE AUTONOMY

PATTY WILSON

Introduction

Although there are many different types of crochet, including Tunisian, filet, hairpin, and freestyle, this book is dedicated to standard yarn crochet. Common items crocheters make with this type of crochet include sweaters, hats, mittens, scarves, afghans, and home accessories—but the only limit is a fiber artist's imagination.

The author of this eye-opening book aims to share her knowledge and passion on the subject and aims to help more and more people to learn crochet in a simple and fast way so you can play in complete autonomy this extraordinary hobby. This is a complete guide to Crocheting and inside this book, you will find modern crochet projects as you know crochet is increasingly fashionable and even designers have garments made with crochet in their parades. Before a person starts crocheting, he or she may want to begin by learning some basics. The best way to begin is to know what a row and a single crochet are. Then, the first step in basic crochet instructions will be to get a few simple supplies of crochet.

To start any crochet project, it is necessary to do a slipped node with the loop on your crochet hook. This can be achieved by forming a loop and holding it in your left hand between your thumb and forefinger. Push the yarn through the loop with the crochet hook in your right hand, and then bring the thread through for a second time. Pull the thread tightly at the bottom of the loop at this time, and you will be able to start crocheting.

Of course, these are just the basic crochet instructions and you will learn about a lot more stitches. Every crochet pattern has its own stitches, so it is much easier to learn after you learn the basic stitches.

Learning to crochet is a skill that you will find useful because you can take what you learn and turn it into garments and projects that provide joy and utility for people who use them. There is a large variety of uses for the crochet stitches covered in this book. With your imagination, you can take your new knowledge of the stitches and create your own patterns and designs to make a variety of projects of your own.

Chapter 1: Crochet Basics (Tools, How to hold hook, and Yarn)

Hook

A crochet hook is practically the most important tool of all. Having no hook is like having no camera to take pictures. This tool allows you to create loops in the yarn and interlock these loops into stitches. The crochet hook has a pointy hook end to make it easier for you to insert yarns and hook them. It also has a slanted groove underneath that enables folks to pull loops through easily.

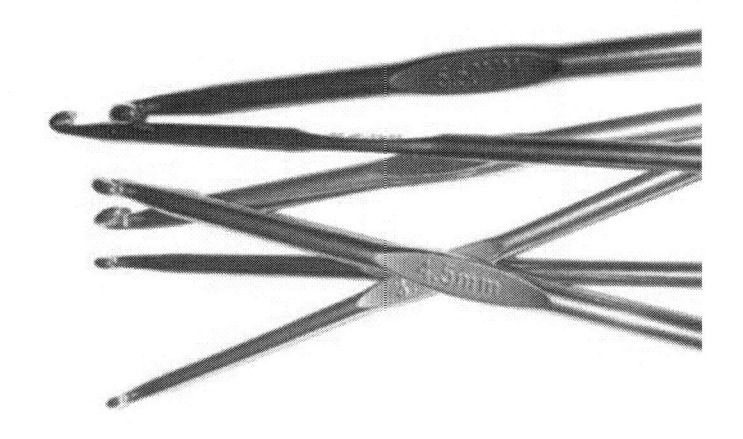

These hooks are made using a variety of materials with the most common being aluminum, wood, and plastic. They also come in various sizes depending on the kind of yarn you're using. For beginners, it is recommended you start crocheting using a basic aluminum crochet hook that is mid-range in size. This allows the beginner to acquire greater control when stitching and looping.

Crochet hooks are typically made of wood, plastic, casein, or metal. They are designed for right or left-handed use and the handles are all shaped in different ways for comfort, ease of use, or personal preference.

Below are a few examples of what is currently on the market (*shown from left to right in the image below*):

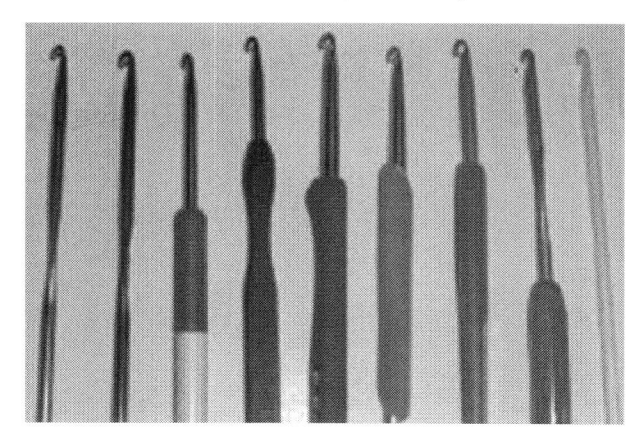

- **Generic Aluminum Hook**—these hooks are generally not inline and cheap, which can be problematic if you need something sturdy. Always consider thickness when buying one of these.

- **Boye Hook**—these hooks are also not inline, and are the most commonly referred to when talking about styles. They are very popular, most people who love to crochet have a selection in different sizes.
- **Addi Comfort Grip Hook**—these hooks are designed with comfort in mind. The shorter handle means less to work with. Addi is a European manufacturer so their products are typically found online.
- **Kollage Square Hook**—these are rounded, not inline hooks which are aimed at people who prefer to work with the hook in the knife grip. Kollage is American-made and available in a range of different sizes and shapes.
- **Tulip Etimo Hook**—these hooks are manufactured in Japan and are sturdy, sitting in between inline and not inline, making them the best of both worlds. They are more suitable for pencil grip users.
- **Hamanaka Raku Rake Double-Ended Hook**—these hooks are also manufactured in Japan. The double-ended, shorter hooks are comfortable in both styles of holds.
- **Clover Soft Touch Hook**—the head of these hooks is in between inline and not inline. It's sturdy and comfortable to use with a range of materials.
- **Susan Bates Hook**—these are inline hooks with are a great alternative to Boye. They're inexpensive and work well.
- **Bamboo Hook**—these hooks are in line with a cylindrical-shaped handle. They are shorter which some prefer, but others find more challenging to work with. The usage of this depends on your grip and is better tested before buying.

Crochet Hook Size Conversion Chart

You should be aware of all the different kinds of hooks available for crocheting. This will help you in selecting the correct yarn type. Most hooks already have their metric millimeters stamped on them, so it makes figuring out the hook sizes much easier. The hook size must correspond with the thickness of the yarn. The thicker the yarn, the thicker hook diameter you will need. As for thinner yarns, you can work with thinner hooks of course.

Here is a simple conversion chart for you to compare the metric measurements between UK and US crochet hook sizes. This will make it easier for you to select a yarn according to the diameter. Keep in mind that hook sizes may vary depending on the manufacturer, hence this chart is a simple guide for you to get started.

Metric (millimeters)	UK Size	US Size
2 mm	14	-
2.25 mm	13	B-1
2.5 mm	12	-
2.75 mm	-	C-2
3 mm	11	-
3.25 mm	10	D-3

3.5 mm	9	E-4
3.75 mm	-	F-5
4 mm	8	G-6
4.5 mm	7	7
5 mm	6	H-8
5.5 mm	5	I-9
6 mm	4	J-10
6.5 mm	3	K-10.5
7 mm	2	-
7 mm	2	-
9 mm	00	M/N-13
10 mm	000	N/P-15

Holding the Hook

Using the hand you usually write with—your "hook hand"—grip the flattened part of the hook between your thumb and forefinger as though it were a pencil, with the hook facing down. Your thumb should be around 5cm/2" away from the tip of the hook.

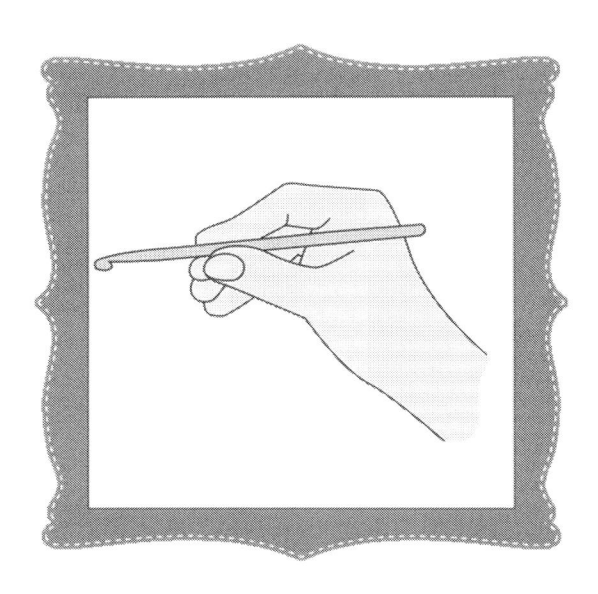

Left Handed crocheters: hold the hook the exact same way in your left hand.

The Pencil Grip

Finding the right grip that you are comfortable with is important because it allows you to work with ease and make crocheting more enjoyable. The pencil grip is the more favored grip between the two types of grip. Just as the name suggests, the pencil grip lets you hold your hook as if you're holding a pencil. This grip can give you maximum control when crocheting as you are writing. It gives the same feeling when you write on paper using your pencil. This grip gives a natural flow each time you hook a yarn.

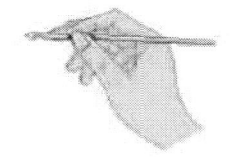

pencil grip

The Knife Grip

Some find it easy to crochet using the knife grip and feel more comfortable using the said grip. In a knife grip, you hold your crochet hook in the same manner that you hold a knife. It is an overhand grip that gives you the same ease and control as slicing something using a knife.

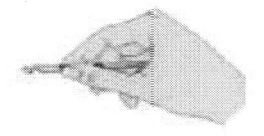

knife grip

More people favor pencil grip, but only you can tell which grip suits your preference—the one that can give you comfort and ease.

The way you hold the hook depends on what is the most comfortable for you. Some people like to switch between the holds to prevent hand cramps or weariness.

You must select the right crochet hook, not only for the yarn you have selected and the project you're working on but also for your comfort. Working with the right hook will make all the difference to your finished project.

Yarns

The second most important item on the list is yarn. Without it, one can obviously not crochet. The composition of the yarn can vary depending on the crochet project. Yarn is typically made from spun organic fibers that are derived from alpaca and wool. Both these materials are great in providing warmth and elasticity.

Synthetic fibers such as acrylics are also used as an alternative. For beginners, you want to use yarn that is easy to work with, so go for yarn that comes in light, solid colors rather than those with multi-colored strands. This is crucial because it will help you distinguish your stitches as you go about learning different types of stitches.

As a beginner, you also want to use worsted weight yarn. This is a type of medium-weight yarn that is very versatile and extremely easy to work with. This yarn is perfect for creating large blankets and small Japanese amigurumi toys.

The yarn is what you'll be using to create your piece, so you will want to choose one that you like, but also one that is suitable for the equipment you have and the project you're working on. When buying the yarn, there are a few things you should take into consideration:

- **Yarn Texture**—smooth yarn is easier to work with for a first project.
- **Yarn Color**—lighter colors are easier to work with as you can see the stitches better.
- **Yarn vs. Crochet Thread**—thread is more challenging to work with, but perfect for projects such as doilies.
- **Yarn Weights**—Medium to higher weights are easier to start with.

The main choices of yarn available are:

- **Wool Yarn**—this is an excellent choice for practicing crochet stitches as it's easy to unravel and rework.

- **Cotton Yarn**—this is an inelastic fiber which makes it slightly more challenging than wool.

- **Acrylic Yarn**—this is very popular as it's available in a variety of colors and it's also affordable.

Holding the Yarn

While your work is down to what feels comfortable for you, but below are a few tips to get you started:

- You place the yarn in your less dominant hand.
- The yarn hand controls the tension of the yarn being fed and determines how loose or tight your finished project will be.
- You can practice weaving the yarn through your fingers to see which feels the most comfortable and controlled for you.

There are lots of ways of controlling the yarn while you crochet, and after a while, you will find what works best for you. Try this technique to start with [a]: The hand that is not holding the hook will be called your "yarn hand." Release a decent amount of yarn from the ball and start by winding it around your little finger.

Next, pass it under the next finger along, bringing it out over your middle and index fingers.

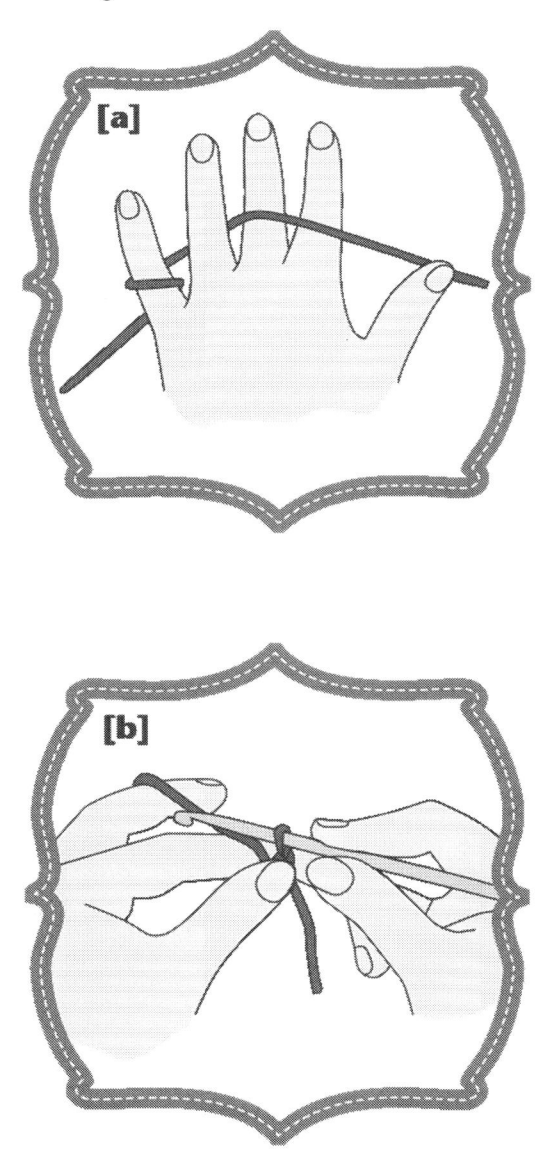

[a]

[b]

Tapestry Needle

Some projects require you to sew your work, and you will need a tapestry needle for that. You can also use the tapestry needle to sew a crocheted appliqué to your project if it can make the project more appealing. The needle is typically larger than the average needle for sewing and has a rounded (blunt) tip. It has a threading eye to accommodate any yarn, although it may not work for bulky threads.

While often used for cross-stitching, tapestry needles prove to be useful for crocheted materials, too, especially if you need to put on more detail on your project.

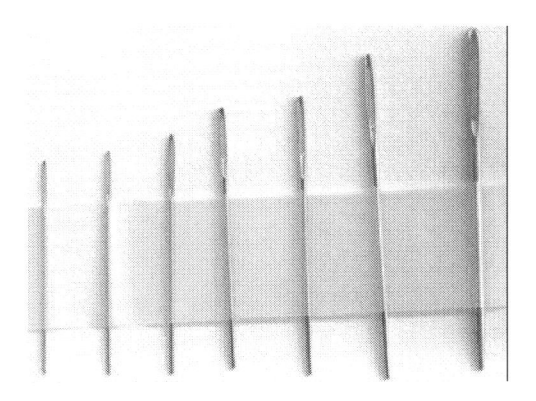

Pictured above are various Tapestry Needle sizes. (L-R: 28, 26, 24, 22, 20, 18, 16)

As you may have noticed, the larger the needle, the smaller the number gets—so don't get confused into buying a largely numbered needle thinking it would be a small-sized one.

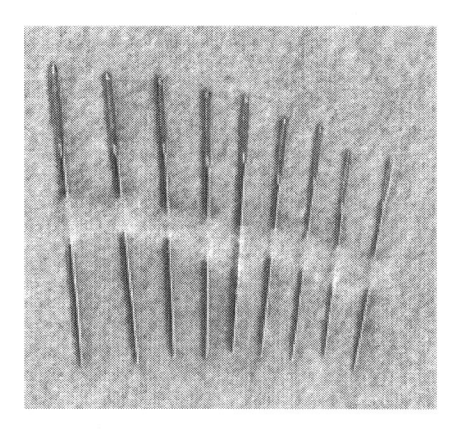

(L-R: 18, 19, 20, 21, 22, 23, 24, 25, 26)

Meanwhile, there are also other tapestry needles called **Tweens.** These are needles that fall between tapestry needles of regular sizes. Tweens are best used for projects where regular-sized ones may be a little too small or large.

Choosing Tapestry Needles

Now, you may wonder how exactly you'd choose your tapestry needles. Well, a general rule of thumb here is to make sure that you use the kind of needles that will easily accommodate whatever yarn or thread you're currently working with. This means that you'd have to use the smallest needle available, but not necessarily the smallest one out of all sizes because this would do nothing good for your fabric.

Scissors

This is a tool commonly used in homesteads for homemade clothes or trimming of oversized curtains and towels. It is also known for being used by tailors for cutting their materials and for another trimming of textile. Scissors on crochet are also paramount.

Just like the hooks, the scissors have their types and different functions on a craft or any material using yarn and hooks. The basic one is the general craft scissors which can be found locally and easily. It is okay to use the general craft scissors on different fibers because it does not leave sharp edges and cuts in a zigzag manner just like the pinking shears. Here, the type of scissor does matter when the crochet is in the completion stage as it helps cut it into nice pieces without producing threads and tears inappropriately.

When buying them online, make sure you check their specifications, as others might not be suitable for your project. The recommended scissors are; standard, snips, embroidery scissors, and lastly the dressmaker. Embroidery scissors could be perfect for this case because it helps cut the exact yarn being used without tampering with the rest of the project.

To give your thread a clean-cut, you need a pair of scissors. It does not need to be an expensive pair, just the one that is sharp enough to cut your thread without trouble. Make sure to maintain your scissors properly.

Almost all craft projects require scissors. You will require it to snip yarn or lose threads for stitching purposes. There are no special scissors for crocheting, but you do want to get a pair of reliable quality scissors. You should get a pair with a sharp pointed end. Make sure the pointed end is small enough to make quick, clean, and precise cuts. Dressmaking scissors are not recommended as they make it harder to cut with precision.

As for crochet scissors, one of the most recommended ones is Stork Embroidery Scissors. They're amazing because they do not leave unhinged threads on your project, and would definitely make your crafts neat as could be. Even stitches in front of your fabric will be neatly removed.

A sample is shown below.

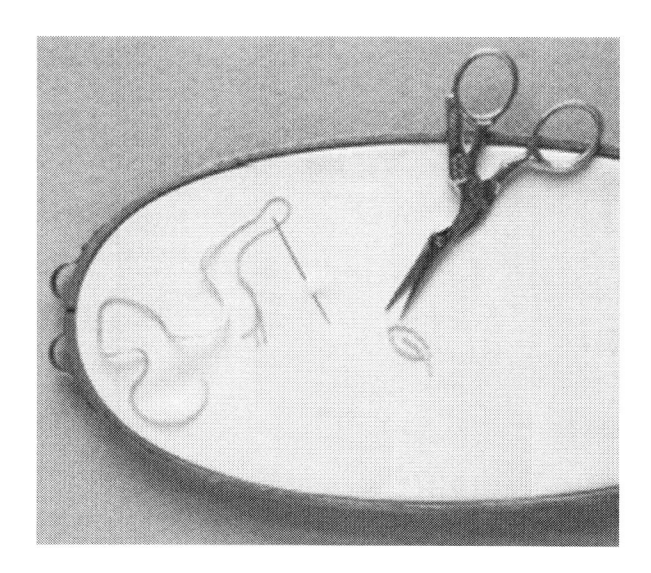

Stitch Markers

These are clips used to mark areas of interest in crochet. There are different designs of crochets and when you have a slightly complex craft, it is always advisable for one to have a stitch marker. For beginners, it is always complicated to make crochets with corners or even rounded by following the pattern. This means the stitch markers are perfect for making areas where it forms patterns unless one is a professional.

Stitch makers have crafted clips that help indicate or put marks on a design to help a beginner or a craftsman to have a perfect and uniformed crotchet.

Any size and type of stitch markers can be used on any piece and type of yarn, as it does not favor the material. The maker can be found in local stores and most people prefer them depending on the sizes of their hands, or how perfectly they can hold them.

The usual stitch markers look like key holders, paper clips, small plastic hoops, and tiny padlocks. The markers are useful in keeping track of the start or end of a round in the pattern with repetitive instructions.

The marker can also serve as a reminder of the number of stitches that you have made so far. You can also use the markers to keep track of the round that you are currently crocheting.

Crochet Book

This is a tutorial book that helps a beginner to know hundreds of designs, both fancy and basic, and it is easy to use. As the name suggests, it is a book that outlines pictorial information and insights on a couple of designs that have been elaborated. The book is essential for a beginner who intends to perfect the art by learning page per page and hook by hook. The book can be found online and one can order it to be delivered to your country.

With the age of the Internet, if you cannot get the hardcopy, there are many tutorials on the Internet of the same type and you can learn from various tutorials that can help you develop the art of crocheting. When you finally get to learn some designs, you can create your patterns and be creative too. Some of the professionals all over the globe started with a few designs and created others over the years which have been adopted by the crocheting community worldwide. This means there is room for being creative and innovative.

Darning Needle

As the name suggests, it is a form of a needle with a bigger hole than the normal needle where the yarn passes through. The sharp end is a little blunt compared to a sewing needle and helps in making a perfect end on the crochet. The darning needle is used to fix the end of each crochet to enable it to stay stable when in use. This is similar to sewing where you tie a knot at the end of the material, but for crochet, the darning needle is used to make the knot, which will keep the whole crochet intact and in perfect shape.

There is no big problem when choosing a darning needle as one can compare with the size of the yarn and its hole to see if it perfectly fits. The one with a larger hole can accommodate every kind of yarn and there should not be any problem whatsoever.

Tape measure

Some of you could be wondering why almost everything that is used by tailors is being used to craft crochet, and the answer is yes, it needs to be totally perfect. Tailors are always seen with tape measures and to make crochet, you might want to get one too, especially for a beginner. The tape measure is simply for measuring and making the right adjustments when following a designed pattern.

This is a necessary tool when there is clipping using stitch markers as it will help to create uniform patterns and with minimal or no blundering.

You have to make sure you make it symmetrical, so the lengths are right. Tape measures should prove particularly important if you are crocheting some kind of garment piece. Including those who like crocheting things like blankets and towels would want a good tape measure available.

When you're actually trying to judge the measurements by sight, you'll be in for a tough time. Both seasoned crochet enthusiasts have ready-to-work tape measures. It makes things as easy as they could be for you, so you're not going to have to wonder if you're doing things properly.

However, for crochet flowers, this might not be necessary as they are very simple and can be modified easily, but it is advisable for big projects and to avoid disappointments at the end of it with different and unorganized sizes.

Tape measures also come in different sizes and types and other specifications depending on the country you are located in. For a clear understanding, make sure you get a tape measure that supports your form of measurements. For instance, America's measurement is different from Russia's and the United Kingdom's. To make perfect measurements, beware of the measurements placed as some may be misleading or have different calculations depending on their form of measurements.

Hook Organizer

After making the first and second patterns, you get to know the stitch patterns and designs that can work for you as you continue to be creative and innovative. The hook organizer resembles a toolbox for a car which is always referred to as Do It Yourself and can work on your car anytime, anywhere. For the crochet, this is almost similar as it carries your essential materials for the work.

After finishing the work, the hook organizer helps keep all the materials used as it has pocket-like spaces for placing hooks, tape measure, darning needles, yarn, and other combinations of crochet tools. One can make any design that can hold the materials with ease and keep them in order. Instead of buying a toolbox for such materials, make one to be among the projects and you will be shocked at how you continue to perfect your craft.

Yarn Bowl

If you have not seen this before, the yarn bowl is a bowl-like thing where you place your yarn when you crochet. The running yarn is inserted through a slot or cutout, so the ball can quickly roll in the bowl without becoming twisted as the yarn is extracted, due to the weight of the bowl. The bowl is ideal to keep the yarn ball from falling to the ground while crocheting.

Row Counters

Row counters come in various shapes. Manual row counters are available which basically keep counting up as you press a button. These are very easy and will work well to keep track of the row on which you are. Digital row counters have become considerably more prevalent in modern times.

Digital row counters operate pretty much the same way, except that they are using an LED display rather than scrolling figures manually. In terms of performance, there really isn't much distinction between the two. The expense of purchasing a manual row counter and a digital row counter is likewise very similar. Broadly speaking, the most convenient way is to buy a digital row counter as they can have several extra advantages.

Unlike a regular wristwatch, you can wear a digital counter on your wrist, finding it quite enjoyable to use and easy to keep track of your row by looking at your hand. It is basic in its nature but in this case, ease of use is a good feature. You can count your yarn's rows very quickly, and it will help you stay on the job. Purchasing one of those row counters may not be entirely appropriate for you. Most people only crochet well without using row clocks, because they are able to keep the count going in their heads. If you thought this will do you good, you can certainly buy one. These don't cost much money and can allow you to keep track of what row you are already on.

Blocking Mat

A blocking mat is something of which you might or might not be used. This relies on the crocheting activities you intend to do. Blocking is a method used in crocheting as well as in knitting. It includes dampening the thread, then molding it in a certain manner.

When you're crocheting you intend to do some blocking strategies, you'll want to buy a blocking pad. It should make that blocking a bit easier for you. It provides you with a good and durable surface to do your task.

This is not a necessary crocheting instrument but you must be aware of it. Without such mats blocking techniques can be used but getting the mats would make it much easier. Mats like that are also beneficial for many other arts and crafts projects. Buying any of these will be worthwhile, and having them around your residence.

Chapter 2: How to Read and Understand Crochet

To pick up or start any kind of new craft or hobby, one must first get acquainted with the language of that particular art. It's the same case with crocheting—before attempting to read crochet patterns, you must first develop an understanding of the craft. This is fairly similar to looking up recipes. When we first set eyes on a recipe, we scan the list of ingredients, the cooking time, as well as instructions to see if it is something that we can attempt based on our prior skill level. It is the same with crochet patterns.

Level of Difficulty

The level of difficulty is one of the first aspects to consider. Almost all crochet patterns are rated either *beginner*, *easy*, *intermediate*, or *experienced*. Beginner patterns are, of course, suitable for those who are new to crocheting as it requires basic stitches that are simple to create simple. If you're a beginner, start with easier stitches and work your way up. Once you've learned the ropes, you can move up to more advanced patterns.

Practice

Like every form of art or skill, excelling at crocheting requires patience, perseverance, and practice. You will struggle at first—this is precisely why you must start with beginner patterns to grasp the basics. But as you continue crocheting more and more, you will eventually get the hang of it and will be to attempt more advanced patterns in no time.

Materials

The materials section is where the designer indicates everything the crocheter will need to complete the pattern. This usually includes the yarn, hook size, and any extra notions or items. Sometimes patterns include the brand names of yarn or other items, but sometimes they merely contain the type of item needed (Lion Brand Fishermen's Wool Yarn versus 100 percent worsted weight yarn, for example). One important item to pay attention to in the materials section is the amount of yarn needed; little is more frustrating than running out of yarn in the middle of a project!

Reading Stitch Pattern Abbreviations

The abbreviations section includes all of the abbreviations used in the pattern. Many times, this section includes instructions for working special stitches. If a crocheter doesn't understand some of the stitches used in the pattern, the abbreviations section is a good place to look for help. Many abbreviations are standardized, so as crocheters gain practice reading patterns, they learn to immediately recognize sc for single crochet, dc for double crochet, and so on.

Reading patterns is not always an easy task. Many of the patterns included in this book will refer to 'stitch patterns'. Each of these 'stitch patterns' has been fully explained in detail, and should be nothing more than careful reading and application to be successful. If you are concerned, try making a small sample of a pattern first if it's something new to you.

Meanwhile, if you have been crocheting for a while now, you should have a good recall of the abbreviations used. Most of these are simple such as:

Yo = Yarn Over

Dec = Decrease

Sl St = Slip Stitch

Inc = Increase

Ch = Chain

Beg = Beginning

Sc = Single Crochet

Sk = Skip

Dc = Double Crochet

St = Stitch

Tr = Treble Crochet

Sp = Space

Hdc = Half-Double Crochet

Rnd = Round

Cl = Cluster

P = Picot

Lk = Lover's Knot

Ws = Wrong Side

Pat = Pattern

Since we will be working with cable stitches in this book, there will be additional abbreviations that you will need to become familiar with before beginning your project. Those are:

BPDC = Back Post Double Crochet

FPDC = Front Post Double Crochet

BPTR = Back Post Treble Crochet

FPTR = Front Post Treble Crochet

Fptrcross = Worked Over 3 Sts

* = Repeat the instructions, or steps, from the asterisk however many times the pattern indicates, or it can mean to repeat the instructions between two asterisks.

( ) = Repeat instructions, or steps, within the brackets.

[ ] = Repeat instructions, or steps, within the brackets.

By paying strict attention to your pattern, counting, and by pulling out anything that does not look right you will find your work will go smoothly. Relax your grip while crocheting to keep your gauge. Have a dressmaker gauge handy while crocheting to keep checking your gauge as you work. Once again, if you find yourself making a mistake, pull out your work to the point of the error and work it again. A mistake or improper gauge early in your work will cause you nothing but problems throughout your piece.

You will find that working a pattern will give you additional options throughout your pattern, which will be anything from multiple colors, to the use of multiple hooks. Don't be alarmed, as once you begin work on the project, it will begin to make sense to you. If you are uncomfortable with a particular part of a pattern, make a sample piece. Let's say, you are reading a pattern that uses a shell stitch pattern you are unfamiliar with making, so take the time to perfect that portion. To this day, I have boxes of tiny portions of crochet that my grandmother made trying to perfect a pattern.

And a word about gauge. Matching your gauge in the pattern will allow your project to be close to the specified size of the pattern. Keep in mind that often the hook size used in the pattern is what worked for the person who designed or wrote the pattern. Everyone crochets a bit differently, some crochet tight while others are exceptionally loose therefore, for this reason, your gauge may vary. Adjust hook size accordingly and make sample swatches for gauge. You will most certainly be glad you took the extra time to do this step even if it does sound like extra work!

Crochet Terminology

- **Acrylic** —Synthetic yarn
- **Back Loops**—The loops on the top of your crocheting work are the front loops. The ones behind these are the back loops.
- **Back Loops Only**—This means focusing only on the back loops.
- **Back Loop Single Crochet**—A variation of the single crochet stitch which focuses only on the back loops.
- **Coned Yarn**—Yarn that has been wound onto a cone-shaped holder.
- **Color Flashing**—This is an effect that can happen when using variegated yarn. It's when an unintentional pattern occurs *i.e.* zig zags.
- **Double Crochet**—This stitch is taller than a single crochet stitch and it's formed by the 'Yarn Over' technique.
- **Floats**—This describes the unused strands of yarn that are carried across the back of the project.
- **Freeform Crochet**—This allows the crocheter to explore the craft in unique and unexpected ways.
- **Frog**—'To frog' = to rip out stitches. 'Frogging' = adding functional or decorative pieces, such as buttons.
- **Granny Square**—This is a crocheted motif that is made from a ring of chain stitches that is built outwards.
- **Half Double Crochet**—These are half a double crochet stitch.
- **Inelastic**—This is a yarn that is slow to recover its shape (or doesn't at all) once it has been stretched.

- **Kitchen Cotton**—This is a yarn that is useful for making projects for kitchen use; potholders, dishcloths, placemats, *etc.*
- **Loops**—Loops are an integral part of crocheting and are created using the hook.
- **Pjoning**—This is using the slip stitch to create beautiful fabrics.
- **Place Maker**—Make a mark on your work (preferably one that can easily be removed) to help you locate a spot later.
- **Plarn**— 'Plastic Yarn' = often plastic bags that have been cut up and repurposed into yarn.
- **Protein Fiber**—A fiber made from protein.
- **Scrapghan**—An afghan created from yarn scraps.
- **Shell Stitch**—Works multiple stitches into one single stitch.
- **Self-Striping Yarn**—A type of variegated yarn which has two or more colors. Often there are long lengths of each color before it changes.
- **Single Crochet**—A basic crochet stitch.
- **Slipstitch**—A loose stitch joining layers of fabric that isn't visible externally.
- **Tapestry Needle**—A hand sewing needle that's useful for adding embroidery.
- **Turning Chain**—A group of stitches that facilitates the transition between the rows of crochet stitches.
- **Treble Crochet**—A taller stitch than the double crochet.
- **Variegated Yarn**—Yarn that has variety throughout.
- **Work Even**—Continuing in the same stitch pattern, without increasing or decreasing.

- **Worsted Weight Yarn**—A medium-weight yarn.
- **Yarn Cake**—A method for winding yarn.
- **Yarn Over**—This is a stitch that involves wrapping the yarn from back to front before placing the hook in the stitch.

Reading Diagrams

Another thing you need to know is that crocheting does not only deal with patterns, it also deals with diagrams. Some people think that diagrams are confusing, but for some, diagrams are deemed to be more helpful than patterns.

What you have to know is that diagrams are mostly used for repeating stitch patterns, creating borders, and even for edging. They're also used to demonstrate differences between patterns, too.

When you are working with crochet, you will be doing a series of stitches in a straight line or in a circle. When you are working in a straight line, you create several stitches until you run out of space. When you get to the end, you have completed one row.

The instructions will then tell you what to do at the end of the row to begin the next row. The initial chain of stitches is not considered a row. It is the foundation of the stitches. You will often be instructed to crochet a specific number of rows in a certain stitch or color. You will also be told the number of stitches included in each row that you complete.

Apart from rows, some rounds contain several stitches around when you are working in a circle. Count the number of stitches around the outside of the circle until your stitches meet, and you close off the circle with a slip stitch. The circle is often started with a short chain that is looped together. Then there will be stitches in a circle either using the chain or the inside of the loop formed by the chain. The instructions will tell you how to complete around, but the round will end when the last stitch is connected to the first stitch of the round.

Row Diagrams

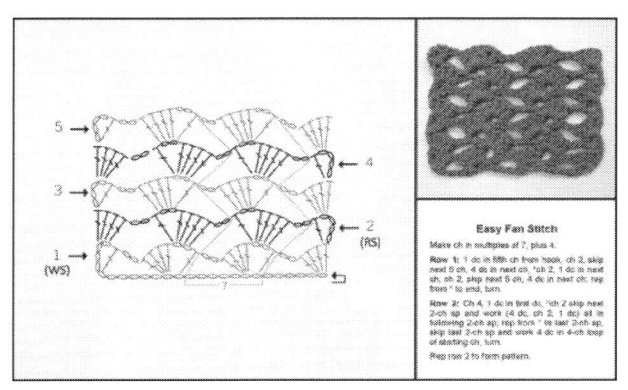

The first type of diagram you have to know about is the Row Diagram. Of course, you could keep in mind that this is used to create rows.

You'll know where to go next by means of following the solid arrows you see on the pattern. Mostly, you start with a straight chain, and then you continue in a zigzag motion, which means you'll have to work back and forth the pattern.

47

On the right side of the diagram, you'll find the number for the right side row. This means that you have to work left to right on that line. Meanwhile, you'll find the wrong side row on the left side of the diagram. This means you have to work from right to left on this one.

Now, you have to make sure that your stitches will appear in columns so while going through the pattern, you'd easily be able to know where you have to go next. Some diagrams also include written instructions. You'll find these instructions exactly at the beginning of the pattern. Basically, these are just "x," "y," and their multiples.

To see which parts of the pattern you should repeat, take note of the bracketed or highlighted stitches you'd see on the pattern. They'll also indicate the number of stitches you have to repeat. Hanging stitches, or chain stitches that hang just by the end of the row shall not be counted. However, you have to count a chain stitch that is situated directly above the row of stitches that you have.

Round Diagrams

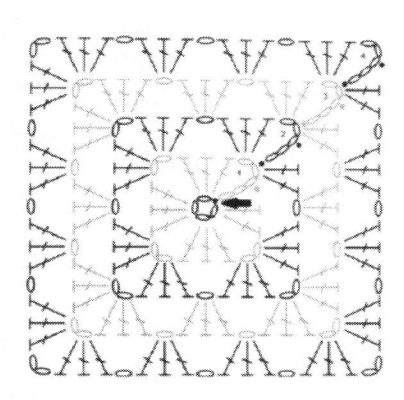

Round Diagrams mostly have rounded edges. Here's what you have to keep in mind about them:

First, you have to know where your starting point is. This is mainly what's in the center of the diagram, like what's shown above.

Remember not to turn your fabric over—not unless you read about it on the pattern. This will only make you confused and would ruin the quality of your work.

Alternating colors and numbers determine different kinds of rounds.

What's frustrating about this, though, is that you would not know whether you should create more stitches, or work on chain stitches. Always refer to the written pattern.

When you see instructions in a bracket [ ] or a parentheses ( ) in your chosen pattern, it means that you need to repeat the instructions inside. Some patterns specifically tell you up to how many times you need to do the instruction inside the bracket or parenthesis, and some patterns allow you to keep repeating the steps (while increasing or decreasing the number of stitches) according to your preference.

Some patterns use an asterisk (*) to prompt a crocheter that a certain step needs to be repeated. The asterisk usually comes with a number that indicates the number of times that you need to repeat the instruction inside the brackets or parenthesis.

Memorize everything by heart and it will flow naturally.

Check the Gauge

Checking the gauge on your patterns ensures that your outcome is the right size. After this, you would also need to count your stitches as you go along so you can keep track of how many stitches there are in each row. Gauge is a dreaded word to even experienced crocheters, but it doesn't have to be. Put simply, a gauge is the measurement of the number of crochet stitches and rows per inch of fabric. Why is this important? Because achieving the proper gauge ensures that the finished item will turn out the correct size. Ignore gauge, and what's supposed to be a cropped, snug cardigan might become a housedress.

A pattern will indicate a gauge either over 1 inch or 4 inches of stitches. For example, a gauge section might read: '3 stitches and 4 rows over 1 inch in single crochet.' This means that if the crocheter works a fabric in single crochet, he or she should have 3 stitches and 4 rows in every inch when using the hook size indicated in the materials section.

Before beginning a project, the crocheter checks that they are getting gauge by crocheting at least a 4-inch by 4-inch swatch in the pattern stitch (in the previous example, single crochet), then blocking it, then measuring it carefully. If the gauge matches that given, it's okay to start the project. If the gauge does not match, the crocheter needs to change either the hook size or the yarn until they get the gauge. This is necessary because small differences in gauge can equal big differences in a finished item: a row of 30 single crochet at 3 stitches per inch will be 10 inches long, whereas a row of 30 single crochet at 4 stitches per inch will only be 7.5 inches long—not an unimportant difference.

The crocheter should generally change the hook size before changing the yarn. If the gauge is smaller than that given (e.g., 2 stitches per inch instead of 3), the hook is too large. If the gauge is larger than that given (e.g., 4 stitches per inch instead of 3), the hook is too small. Row gauge is much more adaptable in crochet, but the crocheter should still aim to get the gauge of both.

Note that with some projects, the gauge is more important than with others. For items with a lot of shaping, including sweaters, mittens, socks, and hats, a gauge is critical. For items that are more 'one size fits all,' a small difference in gauge might be okay—a scarf that is an inch wider than the designer intended isn't necessarily the end of the world.

Maybe you have heard the word gauge and seen it on the packaging, but you aren't sure what it is and why it's important. Well, the gauge is a guideline to tell you what size is correct when you are following the instructions of a pattern. It is offered so that you will be completing your project to the correct size.

The reason the gauge is included in the instructions is that people have natural variances in the size of the stitches. After all, they may make them looser or tighter than someone else. The gauge indicates the number of stitches and rows to crochet and how many inches it should be upon completion.

Finding the correct gauge is particularly important if you are making garments of a particular size and/or if you have to match pieces together. You will want to be sure you are keeping to the correct gauge throughout your project. You may find that you tend to perform stitches at different sizes depending upon your mood or the time of day you are working on your project. Monitor your stitches to be sure they are uniform and even for the entire body of work.

Counting Stitches

Be sure to count your stitches for each row or round. This is important to be sure your project will be the correct size and shape with even stitching across the entire project.

If you are making a rectangular garment with straight edges, counting your stitches will ensure that you have squared edges on the completed garment. If you are working a sequence, you will need to have the correct number of stitches to work on each row while you complete the set of stitches.

By having the right amount of stitches in the row, you can create each series of stitches required across the entire row. This is true working in rounds also. It will be important to have the right number of stitches available in the next row.

Instructions and symbols

The instructions are the pattern's meat, the place where the designer tells the crocheter what to do to make the item. For the most part, designers are explicit— 'Chain 3, work 3 for turning chain, double crochet into the third chain from hook'—but a few common shortcuts are used as well, including:

Asterisks

Asterisks are used to indicate repeats of patterns. A pattern might indicate, "Chain 1, slip stitch into the second chain from hook, *3 single crochet, ch 2, 3 single crochet*, repeat from two to three times, chain 1, turn." The stitches within the asterisks are repeated three times in the sequence they're given after the first time they're worked. So, in total, the asterisk would be repeated four times.

Parentheses

Parentheses are used to indicate repeats, often within asterisks. The crocheter might indicate, "...*3 single crochet, (ch 2, single crochet) twice, 3 single crochet*, repeat from two to three times." To work the directions inside the asterisks, the crocheter would work 3 single crochet, 2 chains, 1 single crochet, 2 chains, 1 single crochet, then 3 more single crochet. Then the crocheter would repeat the instructions inside the asterisks the number of times called for.

Many crochet patterns are also broken down into rows (for flat crochet) and rounds (for circular crochet). Pattern repeats are often made up of many rows or rounds, which the designer will indicate in the pattern.

At the end of the pattern, the designer will include any special finishing instructions, such as how to add embellishments or borders.

( ) Parentheses have information inside which groups more than one crochet stitch that needs to be completed at one time. For example, there may be a simple sequence to be performed like (sl st, 2 hdc, sc) in the next ch-4 sp. These instructions mean to do a slip stitch in the space created with a chain 4 command in the previous row. Then do two half-double crochets and single crochet in the same space. All the stitches will be in one single crochet space. You may also see the parentheses providing additional information regarding the row or round in which you are working. These are often shown in italics; (*54, sl st, ch 3, sl st*) indicates that there should be 54 of the series, slip stitch, chain 3, slip stitch. It is simply telling you how many there should be in the row. The parentheses break up the various directions and groups them together so you can tell what needs to be done in a specific row or round.

[ ] Brackets are an indication of something that will be repeated. The number of times to repeat will be outside of the brackets. It will say, for example, [sc, dc, sc in ch-1 sp] 12 times. This will mean doing the series, sc-dc-sc in a chain-one space in the row for twelve chain-one spaces. A series of stitches form a pattern that will add variety to any project. There may also be items bold and in brackets that indicate a different number of rows or stitches due to variations in size. This looks like *Rounds 14-15 [16-17, 16-18]*. The numbers in

the brackets signify the rounds that will be affected for the large sizes when the pattern is for more than one size.

{} Between the braces, you will find instructions that will be repeated in the same way as brackets. These will sometimes be used inside of parentheses or brackets if there is a repeated action within a repeated action. The braces isolate a particular action to be repeated. [hdc in next sc, ch-4, skip dc, {sc in next 11 ch}] 14 times. This is moving into territory beyond beginners.

* The most common symbol you will probably see in patterns is the asterisk. The asterisk is used to indicate the start of a sequence. Typically, it will be followed by instructions to do the sequence from the start and how many times to repeat it. Take a look at this sequence *sc in next dc, dc in next ch-4 space, hdc next12 dc, rep from * to end of the row, ending with dc.

This is a lot of information, but you will notice that most of the patterns are not too difficult to understand. The ability to read and understand patterns will go a long way to being able to complete fun and useful projects.

Chapter 3: Basic Stitches

Making a Slip Knot

All crochet work begins with a slip knot which acts as your first stitch and can be tightened or loosened easily.

Step 1: First make a loop, about 15cm in from the tail end of the yarn.

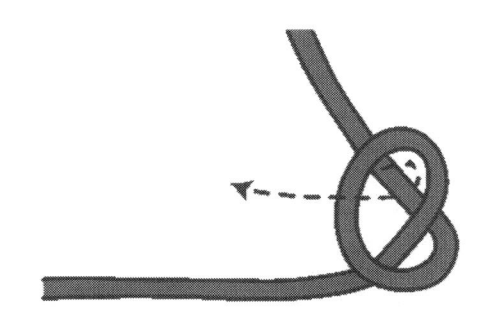

Step 2: Now pull the "working" end of the yarn (the yarn that leads to the ball) through the loop.

Step 3: This new loop is now your slip knot.

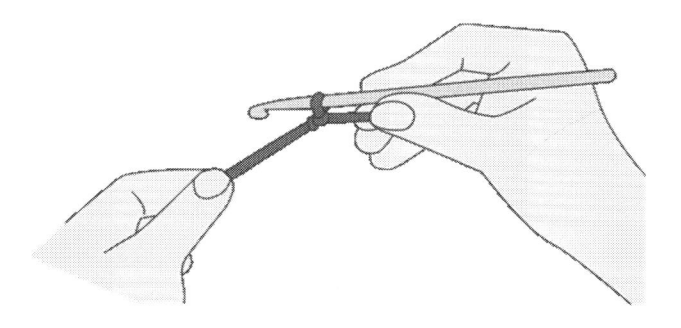

Step 4: Now slip your crochet hook through this loop and pull gently on both ends of the yarn to tighten the loop. It should still be able to move freely up and down your hook, otherwise, it is too tight.

Single Crochet (sc)

Make 11 chain stitches as a base.

1. Slip your hook into the 2nd chain (see below).

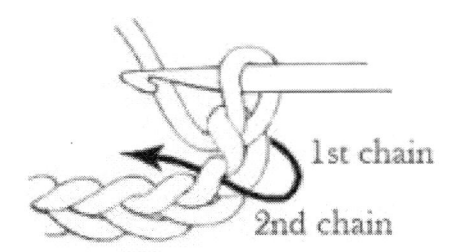

2. Yarn over and hook the thread through the same chain. You now have two loops around your hook.

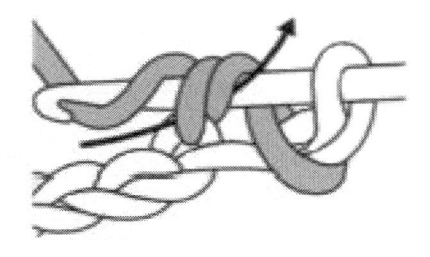

3. Yarn over once more and hook the thread through the two loops around your hook. You have a single crochet stitch.

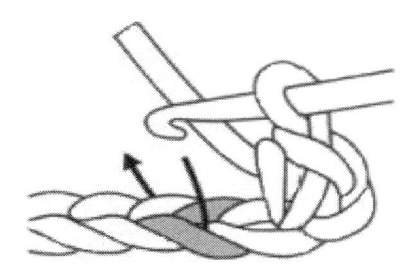

4. Slip your hook into the next chain and yarn over. Hook the thread through the same chain and you should have two loops around your hook.
5. Do steps 3 and 4 again, and do this up to the last chain.

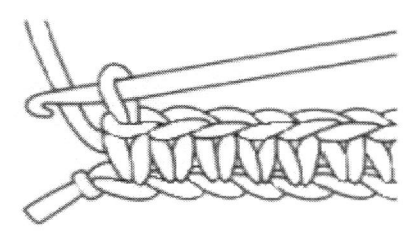

You can make a longer base chain if you want to practice more.

Half Treble Stitch

Once you are working double crochet stitches with confidence, you're ready to try Half Treble Stitch! The result is not quite as dense as double crochet, so it is slightly softer, and is ideal for warm clothing and baby/children's clothes and accessories.

To practice the stitch, let's start with a chain (ch) of 15 stitches.

Step 1: First, wrap the yarn over the hook (yrh) before you go into the chain. Then insert your hook into the third chain along from the hook. Yarn over hook (yrh) again, then pull through the chain.

Step 2: You now have three loops on your hook.

Step 3: Yarn over hook (yrh) and pull your hook through all three stitches.

Step 4: You now have one loop on your hook and have completed your first half treble crochet stitch!

Step 5: Continue by working a half treble stitch into each chain until you reach the end.

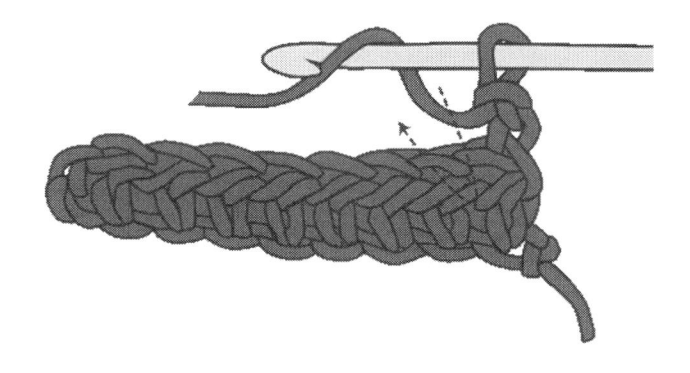

Step 6: As you did in double crochet, now make a "turning chain"—for this stitch you need to chain 2 (ch 2) before each new row. Now turn your work around so that you are ready to begin the next row. Then it's yarn over hook (yrh), slip your hook under the very next stitch, yarn over hook (yrh), pull through all three stitches, and so on.

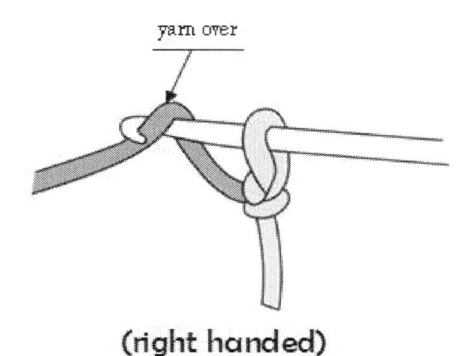

yarn over

(right handed)

Turning Chain

The turning chain is always the first stitch each time you start another round. When the next round starts with a slip stitch, then you don't need a turning chain and it is the only stitch where a turning chain is not needed.

The height of the different basic stitches varies, and your turning chain should have the same height as the stitch being asked by the pattern. See the figure below as your reference.

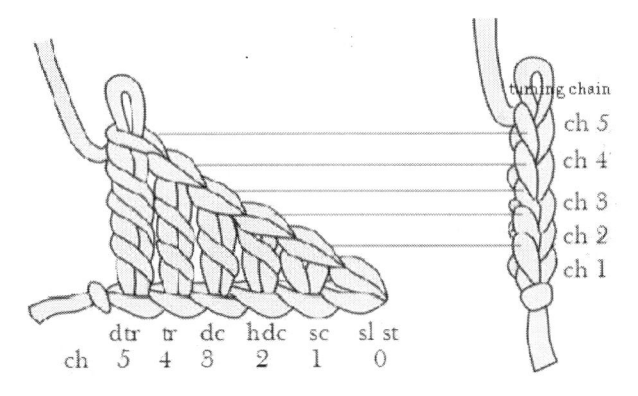

- Slip stitch does not require a turning chain.
- Single crochet needs 1 chain stitch as a turning chain.
- Half double crochet needs 2 chain stitches as a turning chain.
- Double crochet needs 3 chain stitches as a turning chain.
- Treble crochet needs 4 chain stitches as a turning chain.
- Double treble crochet needs 5 chain stitches as a turning chain.

If you are working in rows (not in circles), make sure to always turn your work in the same direction (see figure 1) when adding a row.

If you started turning your work to the right, then see to it to always turn your work to the right each time you add a row. Proceed with your work.

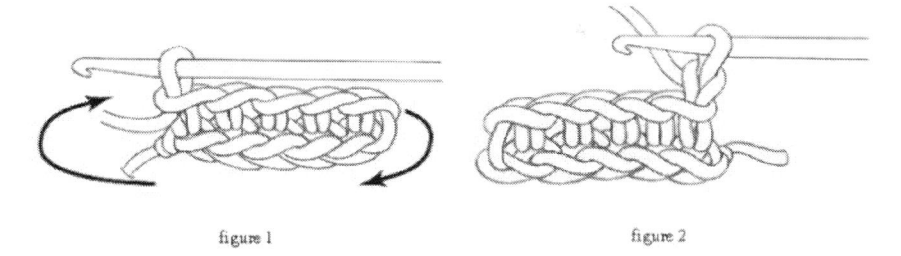

figure 1

figure 2

Double Crochet Stitch

Double crochet is one of the easiest crochet stitches to do, and many of the projects in this book will use this to help get you started. It creates quite a chunky, dense pattern, so is ideal for winter accessories and toys.

To practice the stitch, let's start with a chain (ch) of 15 stitches.

Step 1: You should see the two strands—the 'V'—of the stitch on top of your hook. Wrap the yarn over the hook (yrh), then pull through the chain. You will now have two loops on your hook.

Step 2: Yarn over hook (yrh), then pull through both stitches.

Step 3: You now have one loop on your hook and have completed your first double crochet stitch!

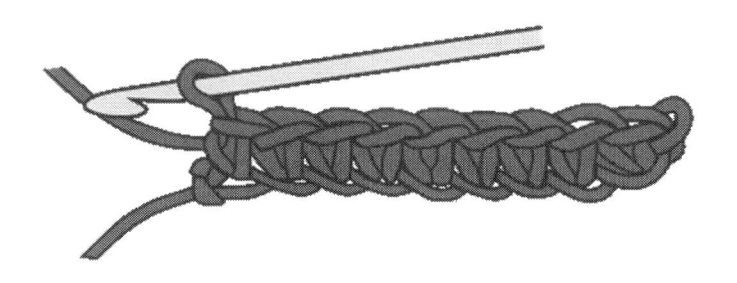

Step 4: Continue by working a double crochet stitch into each chain until you reach the end. Count to ensure you now have 14 stitches.

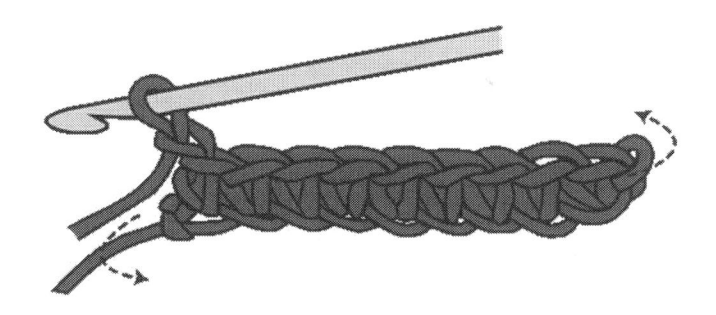

Step 5: Now make a "turning chain" by chaining one stitch (ch 1), then turning your work around so that you are ready to begin the next row. (Most crochet stitches will have a very crucial "turning chain" of one or more stitches, which will depend on the height of the stitch, that you must do at the start of each new row.)

Step 6: Start the next row by inserting your hook under the top two threads of the next stitch along, then continue to double crochet to the end again. Then check the number of stitches—at first, it can be easy to miss the final stitch in the row!

Half Double Crochet (hdc)

Make 12 chain stitches as a base.

1. Yarn over to produce two loops around your hook. Insert your hook into the 3rd chain (see below).

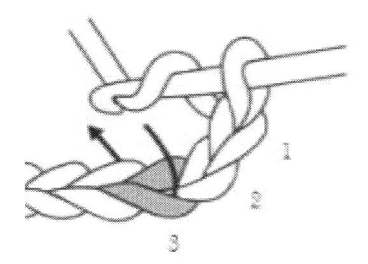

2. Yarn over and hook a thread through the same chain. You now have three loops around your hook.

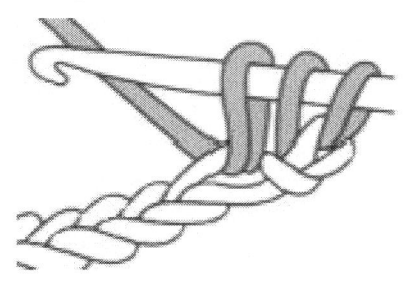

3. Yarn over and hook the thread through the three loops. Now you have a half-double crochet stitch.

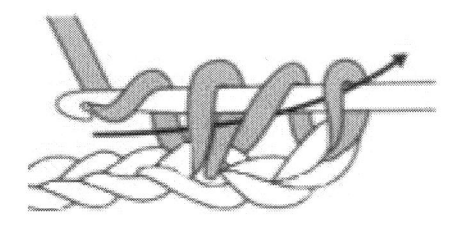

4. Yarn over to produce two loops around your hook. Slip your hook into the next chain, yarn over, and hook a thread through that same chain. You now have three loops around your hook.

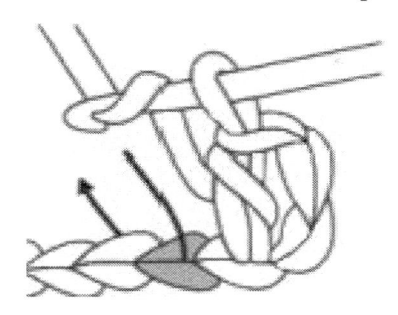

5. Do steps 3 and 4 again, and keep doing this up to the last chain.

Chain Stitch

Chain stitch is the first, and most basic, of all crochet stitches. Most crochet patterns will begin by creating a certain number of chain stitches.

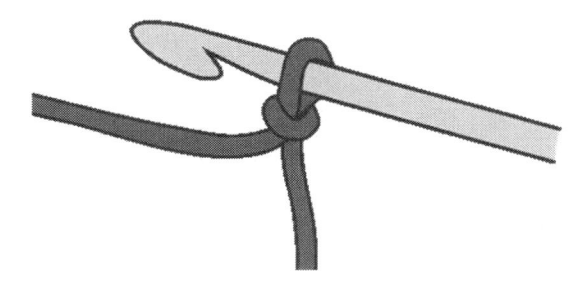

Step 1: Hands in the starting position, slip knot on hook.

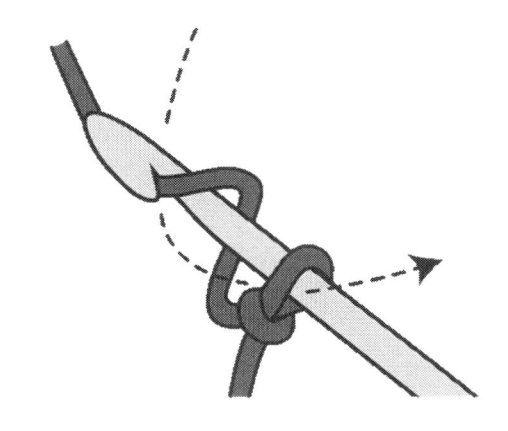

Step 2: Yarn over hook, pull through to create 1 chain.

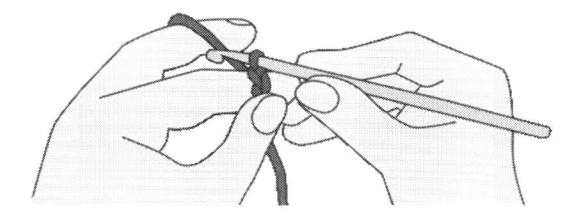

Step 3: Gently pinch the chain stitch you've just made, and repeat.

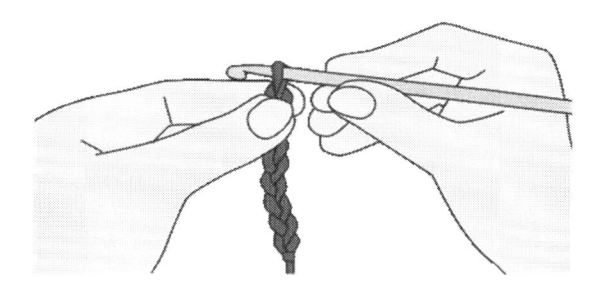

Step 4: Continue as above until you have counted the correct number of chain stitches. The slip stitch does not count. Lost track? See below for how to count chain stitches.

Treble Crochet

Continuing our journey through the main stitches, it is time to learn the treble crochet. Treble crochet is another key basic stitch that you are likely to need for several crochet projects. Trebles can either stand alone or, like all other basic stitches, can be fused with other ones to make pleasing stitch patterns. Trebles are versatile and can be used in every way imaginable. They also work in numerous configurations, such as triangles, circles, squares, rows, and many other shapes. You can use them in almost any thread or yarn, which means you can try practically any material. No need to say that new material must be experimented in a later stage of your learning experience.

You can begin your crocheting from a starting chain. Alternatively, there are many ways you can get started. We will consider the start of our work from a chain for now.

Instructions:
Your chain should be 3 more chains than the number of triple stitches the pattern needs.

Skip the first 4 chains—they are turning chains. Your hook is already through the single loop you have in your chain. YA twice. YO through the chain.

YO and draw it through the two loops currently on the hook (3 loops still on the hook). YO and draw it through two loops on hook (2 loops remaining on hook). Yarn over, draw yarn through the remaining loops on the hook and you've completed one triple crochet (see image below).

YO twice, insert the hook into the middle of the next stitch, YO, and draw it through the stitch (YO, draw through hoops on hook) 3 times. Repeat until you get to the end of the chain. Now you are ready to begin the second row.

To begin, you must turn your work. Start by chaining four (turning chain). Skip the first treble (we talked about it in the beginning). YO twice. On the next triple crochet, insert the hook from the front to the back under the top 2 loops and repeat 3 times. Your first triple crochet is now done. Repeat this step in each treble until you reach the end.

Double Treble Crochet (dtr)

Make 15 chain stitches as a base.

1. Yarn over three times and you have four loops around your hook. Insert your hook into the 6th chain.

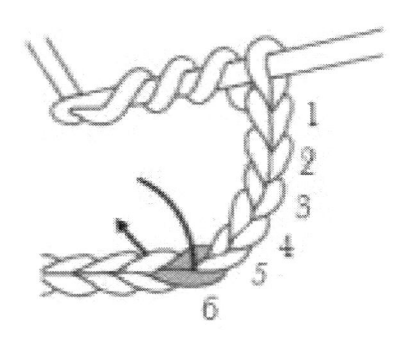

2. Yarn over and hook a thread through the same chain. You should produce five loops around your hook.

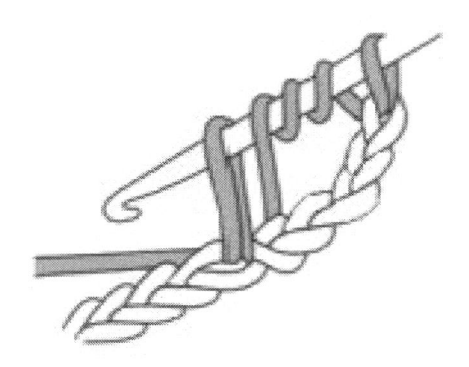

73

3. Yarn over and hook a thread through the two loops around the hook and four loops still remain around your hook. Yarn over again, and hook a thread through the two loops, and three loops still remain around your hook. Yarn over, and hook a thread through the two loops, and two loops still remain around your hook. Yarn over for the last time, and hook a thread through the two loops and you will get a double treble crochet stitch.

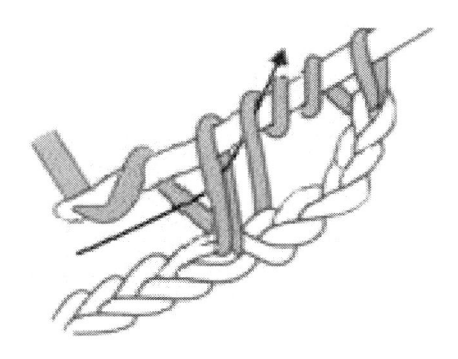

4. Yarn over thrice and you have four loops around your hook. Insert your hook into the next chain, and do step 2.
5. Do steps 3 and 4 until there's no more base chain to work on.

Parts of the Crochet Stitch

Take note of the different parts of the crochet stitch. Some patterns require you to work only on the front or back loop. Some patterns require you to do a back post or front post.

Chapter 4: Beginner Patterns and Projects

Now that you know the stitches, you are ready to move on to the patterns! This is a very exciting time for anyone who is learning how to crochet, and I am sure you are eager to begin.

These are incredibly easy patterns that make beautiful projects, so have fun with these to start with. They are the best way to get used to the feel of crochet, yet give you something that you can have fun with and hang on to.

What makes these patterns even better is that you can mix and match the stitches you use in the pattern. Try making one that calls for single crochet with a double crochet stitch. Try making a pattern alternating single crochet and double crochet as you go along.

The more you practice with this, the easier it is going to become, and the sooner you are going to be able to make your own designs!

Simple as Pie Winter Scarf

Materials:

- I recommend that you use acrylic 4 ply and a size J hook for this project, but if you want to use a warmer yarn go ahead and use wool.
- Remember to purchase 2 skeins for this scarf to ensure you have enough.
- Chain 16.

Pattern Instructions:

1. Insert the hook into the second loop from the hook, and single crochet all the way across the row. You will have 15 single crochet stitches when you are done.
2. Chain 1, turn, and single crochet back across the row.
3. Continue to do this pattern until you have completed 200 rows, or until the scarf is as long as you want it to be. You can also make this scarf have a better drape if you make it with double crochet.
4. Pay attention to the tension you use while you are working your way up the scarf, and when you are happy with the length tie it off and weave in the ends.

Please note: If you want to make this scarf extra fancy, go ahead and add a fringe to it. To do this, you can use a slip knot to attach the lengths of yarn to the end of the scarf on both ends.

Tie securely, and your scarf is ready to show off to the world!

Scrambled Egg Washcloth

Materials:

- Use cotton yarn in a yellow and white multi-color and a size J hook.

Pattern Instructions:

1. Chain 26, turn, and single crochet in the second loop from the hook. Single crochet in each of the next loops to the end of the row.
2. When you reach the end of the row, single crochet in the last loop, and chain 1.
3. As you are working, make sure you slide the hook beneath the 2 lengths of yarn creating the stitch and work up from there.
4. Continue to work until your washcloth is a perfect square, or until you are happy with the size of the project.

Please note: I recommend in the beginning that you tie off your projects with an actual knot to ensure that they don't unravel on you as you are using it. Also, pay attention to what you are doing about your tension as you work your way up the row.

Cute White Flower

Pattern Instructions:

Do ch 5 and join both ends with sl st to form a ring.

Rnd 1: Ch 1, sc 12 around the ring. Sl st to close.

Rnd 2: 2 sc on each sc, around. Sl st to join. You will have 24 scs on your second row.

Rnd 3: [ch 3, sk next sc, dc each in the next 2 sc, sk, ch 3, sl st on the next sc] around. On the last ch 3, sl st on the second chain of the first ch 3. Fasten off.

Golden Daisy

Pattern Instrucions:

1. Do ch 6 and join both ends with sl st to form a ring.
2. Dc 12 around the ring. Sl st to close.
3. [Ch 5 plus ch 3 (t-ch), dc 3 on the next ch stitches (t-ch included), hdc 2 on the next 2 ch stitches, sc 1 on the next ch, sl st on top of next dc] around. Fasten off.

This is just the start. Keep practicing and try making your own design. Start with simple designs and don't stop having fun.

Color Block Bag Crochet Pattern

Materials:

- U.S. H/5.00 mm Yarn DK (Light Worsted)
- Ultra Pima x 3 approx (Yellow Rose, Pink & Gray). Every color is 200 yards.
- FINISHED SIZE: 4 metal D-rings Darning

This has a single crochet stitch around the tote top and is made from the Suzette stitch for the rest of the tote.

This color block bag is lightweight and easy to hold but is still large enough to accommodate anything you need.

Pattern Instructions:

Pattern: color chain 54 A

Row 1: hook sc second row. Sc across the row in each thread.

Row 2–4: Sc across the row in each thread. Ch 1 and turn.

Rows 5–18: Sc, dc on the first row, sc, dc on the next line, skip the row, and repeat to the end, and end up with one crochet in the last line.

Row 19–36: Color shift B. Sc, dc in the first stitch, * sc, dc to next stitch, skip a stitch and repeat until done, ending in the last stitch with one crochet.

Row 37–75: Color shift C. Sc, dc in the first stitch, * sc, dc to next stitch, skip a stitch and repeat until done, ending in the last stitch with one crochet.

Row 76–92: Color shift B. Sc, dc in the first stitch, * sc, dc to next stitch, skip a stitch and repeat until done, ending in the last stitch with one crochet.

Row 93–106: Color A transition. Sc, dc in the first stitch, * sc, dc to next stitch, skip a stitch and repeat until done, ending in the last stitch with one crochet.

Row 107–110: Sc in each row stitch.

Cut the yarn, tissue in the ends.

This color block bag is lightweight and easy to hold but is still large enough to accommodate anything you need.

Finishing:

Fold the finished rectangle in half and seam up the two edges (the mattress stitch was used for attaching the bag edges).

Sew d-rings on the bag, using color A, approx. 1/2 "from the bag tip.

For each handle, crochet 2 i-cords. Through handle should be 18" long or as long as you want. Stable the D-ring i-cord with a double knot. If you do not know how to build an i-cord, check this helpful tutorial here.

Highland Ridge Pillow Free Crochet

Materials:

- Product US model K/10.5 (6.5 mm) crochet hook or crochet model to get gauge
- Yarn needle
- Scissors
- 18"pillow inserts (which are possible to buy or use my tutorial to make your own!)

A pattern in rows to help you figured it out.

1. Ch 2 will register as 1 FPdc at the beginning of even-numbered rows. Ch 2 is counted as 1 dc at the beginning of odd-numbered rows.
2. Job pattern for two parts twice.

Pattern Instructions:

Row 1 (RS): ch 48, 1 dc in 3rd ch from hook (1st ch counts as 1 dc), and 47 dc in each ch.

Row 2: Ch 2 (rate 1 FPdc) & switch, 1 FPdc per st in size—47 FPdc.

Row 3: Ch 2 (counts 1 ft.) & transform 1 foot in every st—47 foot.

Row 4–31: Rows 2–3 repeats.

Row 32: Section 2 repeats.

After row 32, add the first piece. After row 32, do not tighten and continue to finish the directions.

Finishing:

Keep the two pieces to reach the damaged ends. Continuing where you left the second piece at the end of row 32: ch 1, score equally on the three sides across the two pieces.

Please insert the pillow and continue along the fourth leg. Enter the 1st sc invisibly and fasten back.

African Flower Hexagon

This is one of the most versatile patches you will find in the history of crochet. If you join them together, you can create unique things like stuffed animals, blankets, pillowcases, balls, purses, and so much more. The trick to it is to use random colors to make it brighter and eye-catching. This is a good way to make use of scrap yarns.

The pattern is pretty straightforward and easy to do. Connecting it together and experimenting with ideas is what will creativity and style.

Note: This works well with any kind of yarn, just make sure you use the appropriate hook according to the yarn's thickness.

Pattern Instructions:

1st Row

1. Start with a Magic Ring.
2. Chain 3 (this will be considered as your 1st DC) and next to it, make a DC, and then a Chain.
3. Make five more sets of 2 DCs and one Chain stitch. You will end up with 6 in total.
4. After your last Chain, slip stitch into your first DC (the 3 Chains).

2nd Row

This will be a good time to change colors.

1. Fasten off into the first Chain to your left.
2. This row will consist of Chain-centered fan stitches. Having said that, Chain 3, DC into the Chain Space, Chain 1, 2 DCs into the same Chain Space.
3. Continue until you have 6 of these around your circle. One set for each Chain from the previous row.
4. End this row by slip stitching into your first stitch.

3rd Row

1. Fasten off into the first Chain to your left.
2. Now create a full fan of 7 DCs. 1st fan should consist of 3 Chain and 6 DCs. Make 6 of these, 1 set for each Chain from the previous row.
3. And like before, end this row with a slip stitch to your first stitch.

4th Row

This will be a good time to change colors again.

1. This row will consist of SCs. Fasten off into the second DC from the previous row.
2. Start making your SCs around the previous row's DCs.
3. When you reach where the fans of the previous row meet, make a long stitch, going through all the way to where the fans from the 2nd row meet.
4. Continue your SCs around the fans, do not forget to make a long stitch where the fans meet.
5. When you've gone all around the flower, slip stitch into your 1st stitch.

5th Row

This is another time to change colors if you please.

1. Make SCs around the flower again, but this time, only in the back loops.
2. Take off from the last stitch you had left off, make 3 SCs, and when you reach the "corner" of the hexagon (which is the 4th stitch from the previous row, in other words, the center of the "petal"), make a Chain before making another SC in the same stitch
3. Keep making SCs on the back loops of the previous row, remembering that when you reach the center stitch of the "petal" you need to make a Chain, and then make an SC again in the same loop the last stitch was in.

Coolest Headband Ever

Use acrylic 4 ply yarn and a size J crochet hook. This is where you are going to get a little fancy with your crochet skills, and you can let your creativity shine through even better!

Start by measuring the length around your head (or whoever you are making this headband for).

Skip the first 2 stitches, and double crochet in the next loop. Continue to double crochet your way across the row, until you reach the other side.

Chain 2, turn, and double crochet back across the other way. When you reach the other side, chain 2, turn and repeat.

You are going to continue to do this pattern until you have completed 6 rows. If you are making this crochet hat for a man, you may want to increase it to 8 rows, but if you are making the headband for a child, decrease it to 4 or 5 rows.

This is where your creativity can shine!

You can leave it as is, with the wrapped look, or you can add a couple of decorative buttons to the top of the headband. Whichever you want to do to put your own impression on it is great! Have fun with it and let your creativity shine!

Granny Square

Granny squares are crocheted in the round. First chain 4 and join with a slip stitch in the first chain to form a ring. The first round of stitches is not crocheted into the 4 chain stitches, but into the center of the ring.

Chain 3 and crochet 2 double crochet. Chain 1 and then crochet 3 more double crochet. Chain 1 and crochet 3 more double crochet twice more. Join with a slip stitch into the 3rd chain of the starting chain (the first chain 3).

Round 1

If you are changing colors for the next round cut the yarn and leave a long tail to weave in later. Insert the hook into a chain 3 space and join the new color with a slip knot.

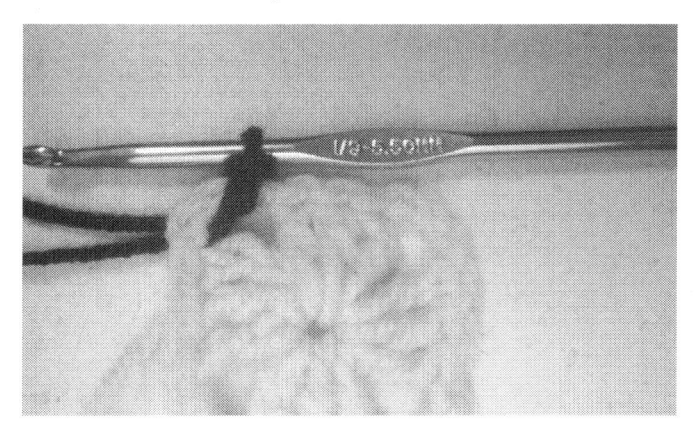

Joining a new color

If you are not changing colors slip stitch to the next chain 3 space. This will position your yarn in the correct space to begin the next round. Chain 3, crochet 2 more double crochet, and chain 3. Crochet 3 more double crochet into the same chain 3 space. This is the first corner. Chain 1, into the next chain 3 space work 3 double crochet, chain 3, and 3 double crochet. Chain 1 and into the next chain 3 space work 3 double crochet, chain 3, and 3 double crochet. Repeat this again in the last chain 3 space, chain 1, and join with a slip stitch into the 3rd chain of the starting chain. You should have four sets of 3 double crochet, chain 3, 3 double crochet separated by chain 1.

Round 2

To begin the third round either join a new color or slip stitch to the next chain 3 space. Chain 3 and crochet 2 double crochet, chain 3, and 2 double crochet into the first chain 3 space. Chain 1 and work 3 double crochet chain 1 into the next chain1 space. Work around the square crocheting 3 double crochet, chain 3, 3 double crochet, chain 1 into each chain 3 space (corners), and 3 double crochet, chain 1 into each chain 1 space.

3 Round Granny square

You can make your squares as large or as small as you like. Just keep fastening off the yarn and joining a new color into a chain 3 space, or slip stitch to the first chain 3 space to begin a new round. If you want your square to be perfectly straight, turn the square after each round and do not slip stitch to the next chain 3 space. This will prevent the natural lean that occurs in the middle of larger Granny squares. If you're only going to make your squares three or four rounds big, you won't really have to worry about the lean. It usually occurs in larger squares.

Baby Square

This is a doily that you could display in your living room or bedroom. It will definitely give your home that classic and cool appeal!

Materials:

- 4-ply medium/bulky yarn in white (A), pink(B), and petal pink (C)
- Hook size: 8 to 5.0 mm
- Square size: 7 x 7"

Pattern Instructions:

Round 1: Use Color A. Ch 3, make 11 DCs in ring; use sl st to join until the top of beg ch 3, and end with sl st.

Round 2: Ch 3, and DC in the same spot. Make 2 DCs in the next 2 sts, and then ch 3. Repeat thrice. Make sure to do 2 DCs in the next 3 sts, and then chain 3. End with sl st at beg-3 ch. This will make 24 DCs, and 4 ch-sps.

Round 3: Ch 3 and then make DCs in next st, ch 2, sk 2 sts, DC next 2 sts. This means you have to DC, ch 3, and then DC once again. Next DC in next 2 sts, ch 2, sk 2 sts, dc next 2 sts. Again, this means DC, ch 3, and DC until you reach the corner. Repeat twice and end with sl st on beg ch 3. Finish with 24 DC, 4 ch, 3 sps, ch 2 sps.

Round 4: Now, use Color B. Start by using sl st in the corner to join, and then ch 3, 2 dc, ch 3, 3 dc in the said corner. **Next, dc in next 3 sts, work in front of ch 2, sp tr in next 2 sk sts, dc next 3 sts)** This means 3 dc, ch 2, 3 dc in corner, and then repeat **to**. Do this twice, and use another sl st to join to the top of beg ch 3.

Round 5: Start with sl st to the corner, ch 3, 2 dc in cluster mode. **Next, sk 2 sts, sl st in next st or ch sp, ch 3, 2 dc in same st or sp, again in cluster mode.** Repeat **to** twice and sl st to 3rd ch of beg ch 6. Finish with 24 dc, ch 3-sps.

Round 6: Ch 6 and dc in same st. **ch 3, sk cluster, dc next sl st, repeat 4 times, ch 3** This means dc, ch 3, dc in the corner, and end with sl st. Repeat **to** twice, and join using sl st from beg ch 6. Finish with 24 dc, 24 ch 3 sps.

Round 7: Now, use color C so you could join the corner with sl st, and then ch 3. This means 2 dc, ch3, 3dc in the said corner. *Now, dc next ch 3 sp, LDC between sts 1 and 2 of 2nd cluster row, dc current ch 3 sp, and repeat until the corner* 3 dc, ch 3, 3 dc, and then repeat to twice and end with sl st. Finish with 64 dc, 24 LDC, 4 ch 3 sps.

Chic Soap Pouch

This one is your simple air freshener—and a way of giving more life to your soap!

Materials:

- 100% plastic canvas/nylon yarn
- Soap
- Hook size: 8.0 mm

Pattern Instructions:

To start, make 12 chains. This will be the base of your soap pouch.

Round 1: From the 2nd chain on the hook, make sc. Ch 3, skip next ch, ch next ch 5 times, ch 3, sc in same st, ch 3, skip next st, sc next ch 5 times, ch 1. Then, join stitches together with hdc and then proceed to make sc so you'd be able to form the final loop. 3 loops = 12 chains.

Round 2: Ch 3, sc next ch 3 loop 11 times, ch 1. Join with hdc in the first sc in order to form the last loop. Remember 3 loops = 12 chains.

Rounds 3 to 15: Repeat what you did in the 2nd round and then fasten off.

To make the drawstring, chain 150, and fasten off after.

To finish the drawstring, make sure that you weave through at least 13 loops, and then tie the ends of the said drawstring together. You may also try letting ends pass through a flaming candle just to secure the ends. Insert the soap inside, close the drawstring, and hang it in your bathroom—or any other place in the house!

Crochet Potholder

Making a potholder and crocheting the pattern in this guide is an achievement for every beginner in the hobby of crocheting. What's good about this potholder guide is that you will be crocheting something that has practical use in the kitchen. In this guide, you will practice making the last and also the first stitch in one row of a single crochet project. I hope you enjoy this guide!

Materials:

- Balls of cotton (Varying colors depending on your preference)
- Crochet hook (size 9–5.5 mm is best)

Pattern Instructions:

Start with the ball of cotton with the color that you prefer to be inside. After this, chain 31.

In the first row, simply crochet into the chain, and in the second chain, start using single crochet until you reach the end of the row (which is 30 stitches). In the second row, after just chain 1, turn your crochet the other way to start the second row. It may help you mark the number of stitches on a piece of paper so that you would not lose count while stitching.

Pick up two loops on top of those stitches, and then simply single crochet again (30 stitches). Once you reach the end, you have now finished the 2nd row. Keep track of the count to avoid any errors in the process. From the third to the thirtieth, after the end of each row, simply chain 1, turn the crochet around and apply single crochet until the end of the row (30 stitches), keep count!

Repeat these instructions until you have finished the 30th row. It should look something like the picture below.

After finishing the 30th stitch, cut the end of the yarn (at least 4 inches of allowance) then pull it through the last loop at the end of the row. Make sure to pull it tight enough and secure it with a knot (binding off).

Repeat all the instructions at the top and create another one. Check the picture above. Use the other color that you picked, by the way. This side is the outer part of the potholder. But remember not to cut the end of the yarn on this second attempt.

In attaching these two pieces, you would need to create the other one having its rows sideward and the other one up and down. This is an IMPORTANT step in the whole guide. If you do not follow this correctly, you would not be able to create a potholder.

The back piece is the last one you have created and the one on top is the first one that you made. Make sure that your crochet hook is properly placed, as in the picture above.

On the back piece, chain 1 and do not turn the crochet around. Observe the picture below. After you have chained 1 you should put it through the two square layers. See the picture below.

The picture below shows how you should put it through the two layers.

Remember that your hook should be placed between the stitches in the first row for security. A more secure crochet results from this.

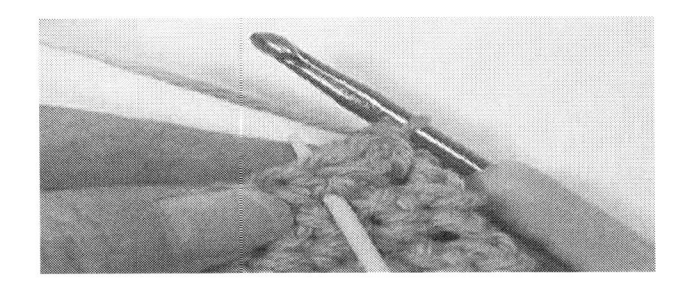

After crocheting the loose ends for 4–6 stitches, it is time to pull it a little to secure the whole row. Make sure not to pull it too tightly, though.

Slowly crochet along the edges of the squares. Be precise in stitching one layer to another row. Slowly bring the two squares together. You can also count the number of stitches from time to time and compare them to the rows. Make sure that you have not missed a single stitch in the process.

When you get to the corner, single crochet 3 times to create stitches on the same corner. This would allow you to properly place your crochet hook and allow it to move to the next side. Keep going on the other side and pick up row by row and stitch by stitch until the end. Repeat the process.

The picture shows loose ends (2, in fact). Simply go around both by single crocheting around 4–6 stitches. Pull the short end to make the whole structure secure. Don't forget to push the end between the two square layers. Keep going until the last loose end and repeat the process of single crocheting 4–6 stitches and pulling to secure.

Now on the third side, repeat the process of single crochet 3 around the corner and continue to the last side.

Single crochet then chains 6 more stitches and skip 2 stitches which would then lead to you slip stitching into the third one.

Now it's time to cut the yarn. Pull it and make a knot, making sure that it's secured well.

Hiding the thread that remains is easy. Simply put your crochet hook at the top and pull it inside to hide it. Make sure that it ends up inside the two square layers.

Congratulations! You have now created your own crochet potholder. You can use this to hold your pot and other hot utensils used for cooking since it has a very heat-resistant property that would prevent you from burning.

Fall Crochet Bunting

Materials:

- Size 4 yarn in 2 colors: size J/6.0 mm
- Crochet hook
- Yarn
- Needle scissors

Gauge: 4 "size = 13 dc finished size: each rectangle has 4.5" long x 6.25 'tall designs. I prefer to crochet tightly. Since this is not a wearable object, if your size varies and your rectangles turn out to be slightly larger or smaller than mine, it will not be as big a deal.

However, if you crochet looser than me, your rectangles can be a little more "floppy" than mine. If so, you may want to down one or two sizes with your crochet hook to get the fabric you need.

There will be slight curling of the rectangles, regardless of what the length is. Before I go on, I would suggest blocking your rectangles.

Growing row's start chain does not count as a stitch.

I refer to the main color of Color A and the complementary color of Color B in the 3 lines.

Pattern Instructions:

Row 1: Use Color A, 14 FDC, or (unless you want double crochet foundation) Chain 16. Dc through the third chain of the hook and through each row.

Row 2: Ch 1. (14) Row 2: Transform. Sc in the same thread and in every line. (14) Color switches B and Color A are done.

Row 3: Ch 1. Switch. Switch. Turn. Sc in one stitch and around each thread. Switch to Color A and full Color B. (14)

Row 4: Ch 2. Row 4: Switch. Turn. Dc in the same thread and throughout every line. Switch to Color B and full Color A.

Row 5: Ch 2. Switch. Turn. Dc in one row and around each thread. Color A shift and Color B finish. (14)

Row 6: Ch 2. Switch. Turn. Dc in the same thread and throughout every line. Color B and Color A finish off.

Row 7: Ch 1. Switch. Turn. Sc in one stitch and around each thread. Switch to Color A and full Color B. (14) Color A completes the rest of the pattern.

Row 8: ch 1. Switch. Turn. Sc in one stitch and around each thread.

Row 9: Ch 2: Transform. Dc in the same thread and throughout every line. (14)

Rows 10–15: Rows 8 and 9 repeat. (14) Complete and weave all your ends.

Note: to prevent your color changing from loosening at the end of each row, I discreetly tied ends together in a small node before weaving.

If your corners curl, I would suggest that the rectangles be blocked before moving on to the next step.

Attach the rectangles: keep together two strands of color A, start crocheting a row. This beginning part of the chain (before the first rectangle is attached) can be made as long as you want. It depends on how your bunting is used. I have wired thirty for nine inches.

Put the first rectangle, together with the two strands of color A on the top of the rectangle (14 stitches). Start chaining again after the last stitch of the rectangle. The length of your chain can be changed depending on the distance between your rectangles.

Cross Body Bag Love

Materials:

- Flikka in Birthday Cake H/5,00 meters hook Tapestry 1 skein Lion Brand tapestry needle and scissors
- For furnishing: fabric, needle, and thread, Faux leather body strap Colour: smooth camel (gold clasp) Design notes 1 Lion Brand Re-up yarn can be used for this bag too.

Unique stitch: Changed bead stitch works as follows: dc, * YE, just insert the hook (as though you operate on a front post dc), pull a loop, repeat three times from *, YO, pull through 9 crochet loops.

Chains do not count as a stitch at the beginning of each round.

Dimension finished: 9 "inches across.

Pattern Instructions:

Pattern 1: Magical ring, ch 2, 12dc in the ring, join to the first ft

Round 2: Ch 2, * block st, ch 1, repeat from at each ft around, add first bead stitch in round (you are attached to the dc part of the bead st)

Round 3: Ch 2, ft in every ft around, join to the first ft

Note: each st will be 3 st-ft, each st worked around the dc, and the ch 1 round 4: ch 2, **block st, ch 1, sk 1, repeat.**

Create another circle.

Join the two circles together by crocheting the perimeter together, while keeping the two circles together with the right sides. Leave 20 stitches for opening.

Change opening by crocheting more to make it larger and less to make the opening of the bag small**er.**

Weave in ends. Turn inside so that the circles are facing outside on the right sides.

Add lining with the following directions.

Add a fake leather strap to either side of the opening of the case, ensuring that it fastens a complete stitch and not just a string of yarn.

Lining the Bag

Lay beneath the bag two bits of cloth. You can do that by piling the fabric halfway around the back of the fabric. Track around the bag, leaving an excess of around 1/2 inch. Label the textile where your opening starts and ends.

Cut out your bits of cloth.

The right side of the bits of fabric will face each other. Use a running point (going back and forth) to stitch the circle while you are using needle and thread. Remember, we added approximately 1/2 inch additional fabric so you could sew this room. Leave the section where the opening was labeled unsewn.

Hold the back of the fabric outwards, placing it in the bag. Change to match the opening of the lining to open the crochet bag.

Fold the fabric carefully about 1/2 inch around the opening and pin it to the crochet pocket. This helps the raw edge between the lining and the bag to be covered.

Tube Pencil Case

We all could use a cute pencil case! Try making this convenient and easy-to-fashion pencil case for yourself or a loved one.

Note: This works well with any kind of yarn, just make sure you use the appropriate hook according to the yarn's thickness.

Materials:

- Needle
- Button
- We will be working around this project in a spiral, so no need to make a slip stitch after every round.

Pattern Instructions:

1st Round

1. Make a Magic Ring.
2. Make 6 SCs into the Magic Ring.

2nd Round

1. Make 2 SCs in each stitch from the previous round. You should have 12 SCs in total.

3rd Round

1. Make 2 SCs in one stitch, then follow up with 2 SCs in two stitches.
2. Repeat step 1 until you finish this round. You should have a total of 18 SCs.

4th Round

1. SC the back loop only of each stitch from the previous round, maintaining 18 SCs throughout each round. Repeat this step until you get to your desired length.

Closure Flap

1st Row

1. Chain 1 and then turn your work over.
2. Make 7 SCs

2nd to 5th Row

1. Repeat 1st row.

6th Row

1. Chain 1 then turn your work over.
2. Make 2 SCs into the next 2 stitches, then Chain 3, skip 3 stitches, and finally SC into the last 2 stitches.

7th Row

1. Make 1 Chain and SC through all 7 stitches from the previous row.
2. Now slowly keep making SCs around the flap and the rim of the pencil case to make it look neat. Slip stitch, fasten off and tuck in the ends.

Position the button and sew in place. Fasten off and tuck in the ends.

Chapter 5: How to Crochet For Right-Handers and Left-Handers

Right Handed

The most important thing is to get a firm and comfortable grip on your crochet hook as this will allow you to proceed to the next step. So, once you have a grip on it with your left hand, you'll need to use your right hand for holding the yarn. This is simply the opposite of what right-handers do.

You choose, as right-handers do, to hold your crochet hook using your thumb and your index finger to keep it in place, or you can simply grip it as you would a knife. Both ways are easy to get used to, so just decide which one you prefer using and learn to crochet that way.

There are, of course, several ways that you can hold your yarn as you work your stitches and that is up to you. One of the most commonly used methods is to loop the yarn using your right index finger. Keep the loose end up and then allow the thread that is attached to the yarn to lie on your palm in a cross manner.

Once you have done that, using your right hand then hold the slip knot you have made between your fingers' middle and thumb. This is the most comfortable position for this. Your yarn will be between your index finger and your thumb, so you'll be able to control your tension nicely using your index finger. Controlling your tension will help you to create consistent, even stitches. It is best to master this from the beginning as it will make a huge difference to the quality of your work later on.

1. Grip crochet hook tightly in your right hand, then place a clever little node on the hook.
2. Place wool over the hook; grab the hook from behind to front.
3. Take the slipknot tied wool and lock. This method helps you to thread a single line. Redo steps 2 & 3 30 times in succession. In the end, you have 31 chain stitches, and one loop is left on the thread.
4. Take out the first stitch of the chain.
5. Then through a hook in the center of the following chain stitch. Take wool from the thread of the chain through the pin. You've got 2 loops on the line.
6. Bring wool on the hook from the back to the front, then pull it onto the hook from both loops. One loop on the hook is left; this gives you the first single crochet stitch.
   Redo steps 5 and 6 with the remaining 29 chains. Make sure that the 29 chains are carried out in the same way. The effect is a full row made of single crochet. 2 people with identical thread and hook may have rows of different widths. Be careful and apply the same constant force to the wool as the hook or else the project will have various sizes of knots.
7. Sew a single chain stitch at the end of each row, and then rotate the counter in a circle mode and hold the hook in the thread. Then start a new row, create the last row with new

stitches. This process gives the rows their form. Research on it makes the rows more illusory.
8. Build a single crochet stitch from the first stitch and in every left stitch of the previous row. Make sure you work to the end of the thread.
9. Cut the wool off the head. Pull the hook straight, take the wool on the hook from the left.
10. Sew wool into a needle and sew from stitches to secure. Okay, that's it. Isn't it easy?

Crochet is quite straightforward. It starts with a single slip knot and it can become several gorgeous and useful things, including a hat, scarf, sweater, or rug. This can be accomplished with yarn, string as well as thread, and also any fiber you like for your project. Learning crochet is the smartest thing to do with a smooth yarn.

Start with the yarn sticking through your right-hand fingers about your right palm up, the end held by your thumb. Tie the yarn in your fingers and back over your fingers before it gets through.

Keep the threads intertwined among your right thumb and forefinger to create a ring, creating a yarn loop with the end yarn of the ball and lift it up through the circle.

Hold the knot, pass your crochet needle via the top of the loop and secure it by dragging the yarn's sharp end. You should've developed a slipknot.

Put it all down before you. Place your right hand below the end of the yarn that goes to the ring, your forefinger about 2 inches (5 cm) from the handle. Wind the pinkie finger around, then under the yarn of the ring. This will provide the tension required to accomplish effective even stitches. Using your thumb and middle finger to twist the knot under the hook to raise your forefinger slightly to relieve stress, grab the hook from your left hand as if you were holding a pencil. You're prepared to crochet.

Force the hook downwards and to the right of the yarn which lies between both the hook and the index finger, with the hook pointing right. Grab the yarn from your hand, and lift it up via slipknot loop from the hook. This is termed a chain stitch (in the guidance brochures, commonly abbreviated as ch).

Learn slip stitch turn work. Insert hook in the top of the loop of the second chain concerning hook. Pull the yarn loop through the chain as well as the hook loop. Introduce the hook to the top of the next chain, draw the yarn loop via both chains as well as the hook loop. Keep going this way until the end of that same chain. You were intended to make ten slip-stitches.

Better understand a single crochet section. Make one chain Turn the job. You're staring at the bottom of your work. Push the hook throughout the top loop from the last slip-stitch produced. Just draw a loop via the slip-stitch. Drag a second loop through both of the hook loops. Reiterate 9 more times now. You've managed to make a row of ten SC stitches.

Do a double crochet piece Ch 2 Turn the job. Flip the hook to the right, to the bottom as well as to the right of the yarn. Insert the hook to the top of the last single crochet hook worked and draw the loop (three loops on the hook). Drag the next loop via two of them (two loops on the hook). Drag another loop via the two of them (on the hook loop). You've managed to make 1 double crochet piece. Reiterate through work (10 DC stitches).

Continue to crochet. All crochet has always been primarily focused on such fundamental stitches or variations.

Left Handed

There are some crochet instructions to follow to start a crochet project if you are left-handed. In most crochet projects the same technique is used as shown in the guidelines below

1. First step—Around the yarn or cotton on the finger, form and pull into a circle. It is like binding a shoelace, and it's called a slipknot.
2. Second step—Make a yarn or 'yarn over'. Scoop your yarn in a clockwise direction with your hook to pick up the yarn.
3. Third step—Draw a hook through the loop. Here, you scoop the yarn clockwise.
4. Fourth step—when the yarn is hooked onto the crochet hook, by drawing the first chain from the top, refer to step 2. The first chain is completed.

Steps 3 and 4 are to be done as many times as the chain depending on the project length and chain width. Hook up the yarn over the top of the yarn and draw it into the loop of the new thread.

For the left-handed crafters out there, you are well aware of how confusing it can be to follow right-handed methods and adjust them to suit your needs. Crochet patterns and instructions are made for right-handers unless otherwise mentioned.

There are so few left-handed crafters, and being a minority, there are not many sources available to learn from. This is because only a small percentage of people are left-handed, and most of them are men. So, when it comes to doing crafts, particularly crafts for women, instructions for left-handers are not a priority.

Most left-handed women use right-handed instructional tools and prefer to use those. They end up learning how to crochet with their right hand. This may be alright for some, whereas others don't have as much coordination in their right hand to create a smooth rhythm. It is also possible to follow right-handed instructions and adjust them accordingly so that you can use your left hand to crochet. This can work, but it is confusing at times and one needs to concentrate carefully.

So, if you are a lefty and you intend to take up crochet as a hobby, this guide should be very useful and hopefully make the process a lot easier for you.

Crochet pattern instructions

1. The rounds and rows are typically used when the designs are crochet. The pattern specifies the number of rounds or rows or the circle and rows.

2. The crochet patterns are given priority based on the work to be done—the difficulty level such as advanced, mid-term, simple, or beginner. Instead of rushing to make any pattern beyond your skill, pick an acceptable pattern with a difficult level, and avoid errors. If your crochet experience adds, trying the next hard stage makes crochet simpler and avoids errors.
3. The number of stitches will start with the same numbers on each round or row as the number of stitches is the, according to the pattern.
4. The number of stitches must be calculated as the size of the crochet hook can be determined. In attempting this exercise- simply crochets, a pattern 4 X 4 inches in size by following the crochet instructions.

When the measurement is greater than the pattern requirements, then the hook will shift to a smaller size or seek a smaller pattern measurement.

Being a left-handed crocheter is a unique thing because you are going to operate against the current status quo of things. This was due to the fact left-handed crocheters had to draw their knowledge from right-handed crocheters. Thinking about this is a little bit hard for left-handed crocheters. You can imagine learning a skill from an individual who does not have an understanding of it. Well, that's in the past.

Today, the situation is different, as left-handed crocheters have a vast number of sources from where they can draw their knowledge from. These sources include various tutorials, patterns, and teachers who have brought themselves to spread the mastery of this art.

When we talk about left-handed crocheting, this is almost as mimicking right-handed crocheting. This is because left-handed crocheting borrows a lot from right-handed crocheting. It can almost seem like a reflection of the other.

The left-handed crocheter, just as the name suggests, will hold his or her crochet on the left hand while the right-handed one will make sure that the crochet is on his or her right-hand side. There are various grips that one may assume when holding the hook. This includes the knife grip or the pencil grip. When this happens, the crocheter may manipulate the hook in whichever way he or she desires.

With left-hander crochets, learning the basics and following the patterns of crocheting is subtle. This is because they are going out of their way to learn the mastery of what they have not been doing daily. Moreover, many crocheting patterns follow the direction of right-handed patterns.

In order to make this less subtle for you as a left-handed crocheter, you need to learn the basis of left-handed crocheting. Below are the various steps which can be very helpful when beginning left-handed crocheting or when maintaining its perfection.

The Hook Should Be in Your Left Hand

Crocheting left-handed will mean you will have to put the crochet in your left hand. This way, your right hand will have the leeway to support the work that you are manipulating. The hook has a flat part that is key when manipulating your work. When you are manipulating the tsk, your thumb and finger should be on the grip of the flat part of the hook. Holding the crochet properly is key when it comes to effective sewing. The grip of the crochet should be maintained and balanced all through your sewing.

Chaining

The foundation of crocheting begins with this stage. When you are engaging in a crochet project for the first time, you will need to practice chaining. One of the less subtle techniques in crocheting is this one. To achieve this, you need to commence by making sure you loop the yarn on your finger. This is often done twice. Your finger here meaning the index finger.

The result of this is what we call a slipstitch. After this is achieved, you will need to make sure that you slide the loop that is on your hook with and loop it too. After this, you free the end of the yarn over the hook. To make another loop, you need to slide a novel yarn all the way through the loop that was already inexistent.

To make sure that the number of chains is increasing, you need to carry out this activity in a continuous manner. This way, you will find that you have achieved a chain. Forming a chain is the most basic stance of crocheting since you are carrying out this activity in a continuous manner. The chain should only be limited to the purposes of your project. When in demotion, chaining is often referred to by the abbreviation "ch."

Following the Pattern to the Latter

Left-handed crocheting entails that you encompass the same patterns that a right-handed crocheter would use. When you have a pattern for right-handed crocheters, you will follow the pattern to the latter only that you will use your left hand when doing this. This also means that you can use many right-handed tutorials to your advantage.

You may be watching a tutorial for right-handed crocheters, but when you follow through with your left hand, you will find that you achieve the same results. As a result, you find that right-hand crocheters and left-handed crocheters are one and the same. The only distinction is that one uses the right hand, whereas the other uses the help of his or her left hand.

Flipping Pictures and Images

Most left-handed individuals refrain from right-handed tutorials not because they cannot work for their benefit but because of their already formed perception about these kinds of tutorials. In order to make sure this perception is eradicated from left-handed individuals, a left-handed individual ought to assume patterns and ways that will work to their advantage. One of the most tactful procedures a left-handed may adopt in a bid to secure a deeper comprehension of patterns is by taking them and inverting them.

When you invert a picture that was taken by a right-handed individual, you will find that it appears as if it is from a left-handed individual.

There are several points to note when dealing with left-handed crocheting. For instance, you need to leave your beginning yarning tail hanging. This should be done at the beginning of every project; its essence is deep-rooted to the instance that you should not crochet over it. The tails come in handy when creating a cue, whether you are on the right-hand side of the cue or the left-hand side.

The right side always manifests itself at the right bottom corner. Another point to note for left-handed crocheters is that every time you are adopting a position of yarning over, you are doing this in a clockwise manner. You need to master this move as this is what makes sense to the whole process of crocheting.

There are numerous patterns for left-handed crocheters; this may involve the written ones and also the visible ones that are visual. Although the visible ones seem easier, left-ended crocheting is possible for both types of crocheting.

This is because a crocheter is being asked to relay what is in the written or what is in the book to what he or she is actually engaging in. A pattern that has been written down can easily be followed through just by the use of cognitive awareness that for left-handed, the direction of the yarn will be a little different. There are various types of patterns which to work best, need to be reversed to be implemented with ease. For instance, there is a type of crochet pattern known as the tapestry pattern that requires reversing for it to work properly. There are also other patterns known as colorwork patterns that require a reversal for them to function properly.

When you reverse filet crochet, one that is used when writing words, you are in a position to read the letters that were written in a manner that is reversed. When a left-handed does not work on reversing this particular type of work, you will find that this creates confusion on the rows and the stitches.

Often, the expected outcome will not arrive because of the mismatch in the various rows and stitches. With symbol charts, this is directed to right-handed crochets. Owing to this fact, left-handed crocheters ought to follow the same drill as depicted in the symbol charts but in a manner that is opposing to the already depicted symbol.

This means that you will adopt the symbol but in the opposite manner. Reversing a pattern can be done in the consciousness of an individual. This entails the individual forming a picture in his or her head and in turn, reversing it. If you cannot do this, the best way to reverse the pattern would be by the use of a mirror.

What Is the Difference Between Right and Left-Handed Crafters?

Although it is confusing to change hands when crocheting, the main differences between right-handed and left-handed techniques are as follows:

- You either grip your crochet hook in your right or left hand.
- You'll hold the yarn in your free hand.
- The direction you work in changes as a left-hander as you'll work your stitches from left to right whereas a right-hander will do the opposite.
- To work the stitches in rounds, left-handers will work in a counterclockwise direction to the right. Right-handers will do the opposite and work their stitches in a clockwise direction to the left.
- Crochet rounds worked by left-handers have a different appearance compared to those made by right-handers. Although some right-handed crocheters think that left-handers' rounds look odd, others actually prefer them.
- Rows worked by left-handers look the same as those done by right-handers, except that the yarn has been fastened off on the other end, so that is the only difference.
- Once you start, you'll have a piece of yarn that hangs down, this is your yarn tail. Always leave the tail hanging and never crochet over it. If a pattern has a right side and a wrong side of the work, your tail can be used to give you a hint. When the tail is hanging on the bottom right-hand corner, and then that makes it the right side to work on.

- Each time that you do the yarning over, you will pick up the yarn in a clockwise direction. This is a good point to remember at all times.

It should be noted that some use "handedness" in knitting to describe which hand controls the yarn tension. Other people call that distinction "English vs continental." Some use the geographical description to mean two mechanically different methods of yarn management: picking vs throwing.

Some people use handedness to mean which direction the knitted fabric is flowing—which needle is giving up old stitches and which is taking new ones. However, as with playing stringed instruments, you don't have to match this distinction to your hand dominance. In knitting, which hand is doing the more delicate operation depends more on the precise mechanics of how you're moving the needles than on which needle is taking the new row as you knit it.

Anyone can use any of these methods and have reasonable success. Some knitters switch from the one they used initially if they find one their hands like better. I tend to teach people to knit towards their dominant hand (that hand takes up new stitches) because in the first week or so of practice, most folks find it marginally easier to poke accurately with that hand, but really the whole set of movements is novel enough you could do it either way.

Chapter 6: Animal Crochet

Bumblebee

Materials:

- Crochet hook of 4 mm
- Scissors
- Darning Needle
- Polyfill for stuffing
- Two safety eyes of size 12 mm

Pattern Instructions:

Body

Starting with pink color

Rnd 1: Make 6 Single crochet into Magic Ring (6)

Rnd 2: make two single crochet stitches in the same stitch around (12)

Rnd 3: Single crochet, make two single crochet stitches in the same stitch around (18)

Rnd 4: Single crochet 2, make two single crochet stitches in the same stitch around (24)

Rnd 5: Single crochet 3, make two single crochet stitches in the same stitch *around* (30)

Now switch your color from pink to black

Rnd 6–8: Single crochet around (30)

Switch again to pink

Rnd 9–11: Single crochet around (30)

Switch back to Black

Rnd 12–14: Single crochet around (30)

Now again switch from black to pink

Rnd 15: Single crochet around (30)

Rnd 16: Single crochet 3, crochet two stitches together using the invisible decrease method around (24)

Remember to add your safety eye to your project unless you miss your chance and mess it up!

Rnd 17: Single crochet 2, crochet two stitches together using the invisible decrease method around (18)

Rnd 18: Single crochet, crochet two stitches together using the invisible decrease method around (12)

Wings

Make 2

Rnd 1: 6 Single crochet into Magic Ring (6)

Rnd *2:* make two single crochet stitches in the same stitch around (12)

Rnd 3-4: Single crochet around (12)

Finish off and leave tail for sewing

Assembly

Now that you've got all of the pieces for your design, all you have to do is tie them up on both the wings, and you're done!

Penguin

Materials:

- Crochet Hook for the main body of size 3.25mm
- Crochet Hook for bow tie of size 2.75mm
- Worsted weight 24/7 cotton yarn in the following colors
- Denim, Ecru, Goldenrod (Each color less than 50g)
- Patons Astra in cardinal or lightweight yarn of your choice for the bow tie
- Safety Eyes of your choice
- Stuffing
- Tapestry needle

Pattern Instructions:

Front Body Panel:

Using a 3.25 mm crochet hook make 2 panels.

You're going to make 2 panels with a 3.25 mm hook. Ch 1 and switch at either the end within each row until otherwise mentioned.

Starting with Blue.

Row 1: Ch 12, starting in the second chain from hook, single crochet across (11 stitches)

Row 2: Work a single crochet increase, twice, single crochet 7, work a single crochet increase twice (15 stitches)

We're going to begin with colorwork over the next row.

Row 3: Work a single crochet increase in blue yarn twice, work the next 2 single crochet in blue, work the next 7 single crochet in white, work the next 2 single crochet in blue, Work a single crochet increase in blue yarn twice (19 stitches)

Row 4: Work a single crochet increase in blue yarn, work the next 2 single crochet in blue, work the next 13 single crochet in white, work the next 2 single crochet in blue, Work a single crochet increase in blue yarn (21 stitches)

Row 5: work the next 3 single crochet in blue, work the next 15 single crochet in white, work the next 3 single crochet in blue (21 stitches)

Row 6: Work a single crochet increase in blue yarn, work the next one single crochet in blue, work the next 17 single crochet in white, work the next one single crochet in blue, Work a single crochet increase in blue yarn (23 stitches)

Rows 7–11: work the next 3 single crochet in blue, work the next 17 single crochet in white, work the next 3 single crochet in blue (23 stitches)

Rows 12–13: work the next 4 single crochet in blue, work the next 15 single crochet in white, work the next 4 single crochet in blue (23 stitches)

Rows 14–15: work the next 5 single crochet in blue, work the next 13 single crochet in white, work the next 5 single crochet in blue (23 stitches)

Row 16: Work a regular single crochet decrease in blue, work the next 4 single crochet in blue, work the next 1 single crochet in white1, work the next 4 single crochet in blue, Work a regular single crochet decrease in blue (21 stitches)

Row 17: work the next 6 single crochet in blue, work the next 9 single crochet in white, work the next 6 single crochet in blue (21 stitches)

Row 18: Work a regular single crochet decrease in blue, work the next 2 single crochet in blue, work the next 13 single crochet in white, work the next 2 single crochet in blue, Work a regular single crochet decrease in blue (19 stitches)

Now from the next row, we will start head.

Row 19: Work a single crochet increase in blue yarn, [work the next one single crochet in blue, work the next 1 single crochet in white] into the same stitch, work the next 15 single crochet in white, [work the next 1 single crochet in white, work the next one single crochet in blue] into the same stitch, Work a single crochet increase in blue yarn (23 stitches)

Row 20: Work a single crochet increase in blue yarn, work the next one single crochet in blue, work the next 1 single crochet in white9, work the next one single crochet in blue, Work a single crochet increase in blue yarn (25 stitches)

Row 21: Work a single crochet increase in blue yarn, work the next one single crochet in blue, work the next 21 single crochet in white, work the next one single crochet in blue, Work a single crochet increase in blue yarn (27 stitches)

Row 22: work the next 3 single crochet in blue, work the next 21 single crochet in white, work the next 3 single crochet in blue (27 stitches)

Row 23: Work a single crochet increase in blue yarn, work the next 2 single crochet in blue, work the next 21 single crochet in white, work the next 2 single crochet in blue, Work a single crochet increase in blue yarn (29 stitches)

Rows 24–27: work the next 3 single crochet in blue, w23, work the next 3 single crochet in blue (29 stitches)

Row 28: work the next 4 single crochet in blue, work the next 21 single crochet in white, work the next 4 single crochet in blue (29 stitches)

Row 29: work the next 5 single crochet in blue, work the next 1 single crochet in white9, work the next 5 single crochet in blue (29 stitches)

Row 30: work the next 6 single crochet in blue, work the next 17 single crochet in white, work the next 6 single crochet in blue (29 stitches)

Row 31: Work a regular single crochet decrease in blue, work the next 5 single crochet in blue, work the next 7 single crochet in white, work the next one single crochet in blue, work the next 7 single crochet in white, work the next 5 single crochet in blue, Work a regular single crochet decrease in blue (27 stitches)

Row 32: work the next 7 single crochet in blue, w5, work the next 3 single crochet in blue, w5, work the next 7 single crochet in blue (27 stitches)

All remaining rows are worked entirely in blue.

Row 33: Dec, single crochet 23, dec (25 stitches)

Row 34: Single crochet across (25 stitches)

Row 35: Work a regular single crochet decrease, single crochet 21, Work a regular single crochet decrease (23 stitches)

Row 36: Work a regular single crochet decrease, single crochet 19, Work a regular single crochet decrease (21 stitches)

Row 37: Work a regular single crochet decrease twice, single crochet 13, Work a regular single crochet decrease twice (17 stitches)

Row 38: Work a regular single crochet decrease twice, single crochet 9, Work a regular single crochet decrease twice (13 stitches)

Row 39: Work a regular single crochet decrease twice, single crochet 5, Work a regular single crochet decrease twice (9 stitches)

Tie off.

Back Body Panel:

The back body panel is worked exactly the same as the front, except there is zero color-work. The panel is worked entirely in blue. Here are those stitch counts again without the color-work!

Row 1: Ch 12, starting in the second ch from hook, single crochet across (11 stitches)

Row 2: Work a single crochet increase, twice, single crochet 7, work a single crochet increase twice (15 stitches)

Row 3: Work a single crochet increase twice, single crochet 11, work a single crochet increase twice (19 stitches)

Row 4: Work a single crochet increase, single crochet 17, work a single crochet increase (21 stitches)

Row 5: Single crochet across (21 stitches)

Row 6: Work a single crochet increase, single crochet 19, work a single crochet increase (23 stitches)

Rows 7–15: Single crochet across (23 stitches)

Row 16: Work a regular single crochet decrease, single crochet 19, Work a regular single crochet decrease (21 stitches)

Row 17: Single crochet across (21 stitches)

Row 18: Work a regular single crochet decrease, single crochet 17, Work a regular single crochet decrease (19 stitches)

In the next row, we will start the head.

Row 19: Work a single crochet increase twice, single crochet 15, work a single crochet increase twice (23 stitches)

Row 20: Work a single crochet increase, single crochet 21, work a single crochet increase (25 stitches)

Row 21: Work a single crochet increase, single crochet 23, work a single crochet increase (27 stitches)

Row 22: Single crochet across (27 stitches)

Row 23: Work a single crochet increase, single crochet 25, inc (29 stitches)

Rows 24–30: Single crochet across (29 stitches)

Row 31: Work a regular single crochet decrease, single crochet 25, Work a regular single crochet decrease (27 stitches)

Row 32: Single crochet across (27 stitches)

Row 33: Work a regular single crochet decrease, single crochet 23, Work a regular single crochet decrease (25 stitches)

Row 34: Single crochet across (25 stitches)

Row 35: Work a regular single crochet decrease, single crochet 21, Work a regular single crochet decrease (23 stitches)

Row 36: Work a regular single crochet decrease, single crochet 19, Work a regular single crochet decrease (21 stitches)

Row 37: Work a regular single crochet decrease twice, single crochet 13, Work a regular single crochet decrease twice (17 stitches)

Row 38: Work a regular single crochet decrease twice, single crochet 9, Work a regular single crochet decrease twice (13 stitches)

Row 39: Work a regular single crochet decrease twice, single crochet 5, Work a regular single crochet decrease twice (9 stitches)

Tie off. Set panels aside for assembly later.

Flippers:

Using 3.25mm hook and blue yarn. Ch 1 and turn at the end of each row unless specified otherwise.

Row 1: Ch 5, starting in the second ch from hook, single crochet across (4 stitches)

Rows 2–3: Single crochet across (4 stitches)

Row 4: Work a regular single crochet decrease, single crochet 2 (3 stitches)

Rows 5–6: Single crochet across (3 stitches)

Row 7: Single crochet 1, Work a regular single crochet decrease (2 stitches)

Row 8: Single crochet across (2 stitches)

Tie off and weave in ends. Repeat rows 1–8 for the second panel. Place both panels together (since each panel is not perfectly symmetrical, make sure they are matching exactly such that the yarn tails line up) and single crochet around the outside of the panels to join them. (Single crochet, ch 1, single crochet) in each of the bottom corners.

Stuff lightly once you have crocheted about two-thirds of the way around. Continue crocheting around, topping up stuffing as you go. Slip stitch to the first stitch and tie off. Weave in end.

Repeat for the second flipper, making sure that the second flipper is facing the opposite direction as the first when you are crocheting around (so that they are mirrored images of each other). Set aside for assembly later.

Feet:

Using 3.25mm hook and yellow yarn. Ch 1 and turn at the end of each row unless specified otherwise.

Row 1: Ch 6, starting in the second ch from hook, single crochet across (5 stitches)

Row 2: Single crochet across (5 stitches)

Row 3: Work [single crochet, dc, single crochet] all into the first stitch, *slip stitch into next stitch, work [single crochet, dc, single crochet] all into next stitch*, repeat from * once more (3 shell stitches)

Tie off and weave in ends. Repeat rows 1–3 for the back panel. Place both panels together and single crochet around the outside of the panels to join them. (Single crochet, ch 1, single crochet) in each of the bottom corners.

Stuff lightly once you have crocheted about two-thirds of the way around. Continue crocheting around, topping up stuffing as you go. Slip stitch to the first stitch and tie off. Weave in end.

Repeat for second foot. Set aside for assembly later.

Beak:

Now use a 3.25mm crochet hook along with the yellow yarn.

Using 3.25mm hook and yellow yarn. The beak is worked in the round by working along the two sides of the base row.

Rnd 1: Ch 4, starting in the second ch from hook, single crochet 2, 3single crochet into the last ch, continue on the opposite side of chains, [single crochet 1, ch 2, single crochet 1] in the same stitch, 2single crochet in the last ch.

Tie off and weave in ends.

Bow Tie:

Using a 2.75mm hook and a category 3 (lightweight) yarn in the color of your choice. Ch 1 and turn at the end of each row.

Row 1: Ch 4, starting in the second ch from hook, single crochet across (3 stitches)

Rows 2–3: Single crochet across (3 stitches)

Row 4: Single crochet3tog (1 stitch)

Row 5: Single crochet 1 (1 stitch)

Row 6: 3single crochet into the same stitch (3 stitches)

Rows 7–9: Single crochet across (3 stitches)

Tie off. Repeat rows 1–9 for the second panel. Place both panels together and crochet around. [Single crochet, ch 1, single crochet] in each corner. Stuff each side lightly as you crochet around. Slip stitch to beginning stitch to close. Tie off and weave in ends.

Cutting a yarn length in the very same color, then tightly wrap across the center. Tie a knot to lock, allowing long yarn tails to be stitched on later.

Assembly

Step 1: Face

First, we have to add and sew to the front panel around our facial characteristics.

Embed 12 mm safety eyes on the front panel around 4 stitches from either the left side. The eyes are positioned between both the 7th and 8th lines, counting Down from the top of the head from the middle of the WHITE rows.

Next for the cheeks, stitch certain pink yarn around a thread below each eye.

Sew between both the eyes and the beak.

Step 2: Body, Flippers, and Feet

Below are the pieces that you must have over this step now.

Cutting off four strings of blue yarn, each about 30cm/12" long, then put aside for later.

Position the two body plates, fitting both sides matched. Make sure you're facing the front when you crochet outwards. Beginning on the left side, at the top of the head, start connecting the panels together by simply crocheting the panels in blue along the outside. Crochet most of the way head-down and stop. (Hewit). Now we have the first flipper connected. Attach the flipper between both the panels (make sure you are using the appropriate flipper because there is a "left" and "right" flipper). Stitch the flipper in position between the panels with a length of thread that you put aside earlier and your tapestry needle. When done, tie a knot between the head panels to protect and cover the yarn tails.

Continue to crochet head and body downwards. If you hit the flipper, single crochet in front panel stitches only (because this segment is already sewn shut). When the flipper is passed, proceed to crochet both panels with each other as usual. Stop down the body, almost halfway. Then, using a piece of yarn you put aside previously and your tapestry needle to place the first foot between panels, and stitch in location. Knit in place again by sewing into all three bits, the back panel, the front panel, and the foot. Attach a knot in the yarn tails once during the place, and conceal it between the doors. Keep on crocheting about. Upon entering the foot, single crochet in front panel stitching only because this segment has already been sewn shut.

Start crocheting around it and perform the above measures at the other side of the penguin for the second foot and second flipper. Start crocheting upside down, stopping at the head end. Now stuff up your penguin. Start crocheting over the top of the head and top off stuffing when you go. Start off with a slip stitch to the first stitch. Tie off once you are done with the stuffing. Punch the yarn tail back within the piece about your tapestry knife. Complete the part with a few carving needles for both eyes. Bow tie stitch and you'll be finished! Rather than using the bow tie as just a bow instead; just stitch it on top of your penguin's head! (Hewit)

Baby Dragon

Materials:

- Crochet hook of size 1.75—2.25 mm or you can choose a hook according to the yarn you have selected.
- 50g cotton yarn of fingering weight
- Polyester, wool, *etc.* for stuffing
- Safety eyes of size 9mm
- Plastic egg
- Embroidery floss
- Tapestry needle
- Scissors

Pattern Instructions:

Head:

1: magic ring, single crochet 6 (6)

2: make two single crochet stitches in the same stitch x 6 (12)

3: (single crochet, make two single crochet stitches in the same stitch) x 6 (18)

4: (make two single crochet stitches in the same stitch, single crochet 2) x 6 (24)

5: (single crochet 3, make two single crochet stitches in the same stitch) x 6 (30)

6: single crochet, make two single crochet stitches in the same stitch, (single crochet 4, make two single crochet stitches in the same stitch) x 5, single crochet 3 (36)

7: (single crochet 5, make two single crochet stitches in the same stitch) x 6 (42)

8: single crochet 2, make two single crochet stitches in the same stitch, (single crochet 6, make two single crochet stitches in the same stitch) x 5, single crochet 4 (48)

9–14: single crochet in each stitch (48)

15: single crochet 2, crochet two stitches together using the invisible decrease method, (single crochet 6, crochet two stitches together using the invisible decrease method) x 5, single crochet 4 (42)

16: (single crochet 5, crochet two stitches together using the invisible decrease method) x 6 (36)

17: single crochet, crochet two stitches together using the invisible decrease method, (single crochet 4, crochet two stitches together using the invisible decrease method) x 5, single crochet 3 (30)

18: (single crochet 3, crochet two stitches together using the invisible decrease method) x 6 (24)

Attach safety toy eyes between rows 13 and 14, leaving 13 stitches between them (count 12 holes). Start stuffing the head.

19: (crochet two stitches together using the invisible decrease method, single crochet 2) x 6 (18)

20: (single crochet 2, crochet two stitches together using the invisible decrease method) x 4, single crochet 2 (14)

Cut the yarn, leaving a long yarn tail for sewing, and fasten off. Stuff the head firmly.

Body

1: magic ring, single crochet 6 (6)

2: make two single crochet stitches in the same stitch x 6 (12)

3: (single crochet, make two single crochet stitches in the same stitch) x 6 (18)

4: (make two single crochet stitches in the same stitch, single crochet 2) x 6 (24)

5: (single crochet 5, make two single crochet stitches in the same stitch) x 4 (28)

6–14: single crochet in each stitch (28)

Insert the plastic egg before you start decreasing.

15: (single crochet 5, dec) x 4 (24)

16: (dec, single crochet 2) x 6 (18)

17: (single crochet 2, crochet two stitches together using the invisible decrease method) x 4, single crochet 2 (14)

Muzzle

1: magic ring, single crochet 6 (6)

2: make two single crochet stitches in the same stitch x 6 (12)

3: single crochet 3, make three single crochet stitches in the same stitch x 2, single crochet 4, make three single crochet stitches in the same stitch x 2, single crochet (20)

4–6: single crochet in each stitch (20)

Cut the yarn, leaving a long yarn tail for sewing, and fasten off. Stuff the muzzle firmly.

Arms

1: magic ring, single crochet 6 (6)

2: (single crochet, make two single crochet stitches in the same stitch) x 6 (9)

3–5: single crochet in each stitch (9)

Cut the yarn, leaving a long yarn tail for sewing, and fasten off. Stuff the arms firmly.

Legs

1: magic ring, single crochet 6 (6)

2: make two single crochet stitches in the same stitch x 6 (12) 3–6: single crochet in each stitch (12)

Cut the yarn, leaving a long yarn tail for sewing, and fasten off. Stuff the legs firmly

Tail

1: magic ring, single crochet 6 (6)

2: make two single crochet stitches in the same stitch, x 6 (12)

3–5: single crochet in each stitch (12)

Start stuffing the tail. Keep adding a bit of fiberfill after every few rounds, stuffing the tail firmly.

6–12: single crochet in each stitch (12)

13: make two single crochet stitches in the same stitch, single crochet 11 (13)

14: single crochet 7, make two single crochet stitches in the same stitch, single crochet 5 (14)

15: single crochet 3, make two single crochet stitches in the same stitch, single crochet 10 (15)

16: single crochet in each stitch (15)

17: make two single crochet stitches in the same stitch x 5, single crochet 10 (20)

Cut the yarn, leaving a long yarn tail for sewing, and fasten off. Finish stuffing.

Spike 1—make three

1: magic ring, single crochet 6 (6)

2: make two single crochet stitches in the same stitch, single crochet 5 (7)

3: single crochet in each stitch (7)

Spike 2—make two

1: magic ring, single crochet 6 (6)

2: make two single crochet stitches in the same stitch x 6 (12)

3: (single crochet 5, make two single crochet stitches in the same stitch) x 2 (14)

4–7: single crochet in each stitch (14)

Spike 3—make three

1: magic ring, single crochet 6 (6)

2: (make two single crochet stitches in the same stitch x 2, single crochet) x 2 (10)

3–5: single crochet in each stitch (10)

Spike 4—make three

1: magic ring, single crochet 6 (6)

2: (make two single crochet stitches in the same stitch x 2, single crochet) x 2 (10)

3-4: single crochet in each stitch (10)

Spike 5—*make one*

1: magic ring, single crochet 6 (6)

2: make two single crochet stitches in the same stitch x 6 (12)

3-5: single crochet in each stitch (12)

Make the spikes and stuff them firmly. Leave long yarn tails for sewing.

Assembly

Head

Incorporate safety eyes after row 18. Position the eyes among rows 13 and 14, and leave 13 stitches among them (count 12 holes).

Making sure you're satisfied with both the eyes being put before pressing the washer in.

Stitch the muzzle onto the head. Stick the face with cotton sticky floss. Stitch the muzzle into the head so that the top section is just under round 11

Body

Introduce the plastic egg into the body after completion of round 7, and ensure that the body glides smoothly across the rattle. In round 5, you might need to increase or decrease the count of increases. Making up the same amount of the round 15 decreases. Introduce the plastic egg into the body when round 14 is complete. Unless the body becomes too short or too long, add or skip the round of sc stitches. (Tullus)

Assembling the dragon

Complete all of the pieces, stuff them out, and conceal the tails of yarn. Knit to the body neck, legs, and tail, including spikes to head, body, and tail.

Stitch that head to the neck as shown in the figure below

Apply a little more stuffing before seam closure.

Stitch the head, limbs, and tail to the body

Stitch on the spikes, beginning at the nose—1, 5, 3, 2 (in combinations), 4 (at the back), 3, 2, 1 (at the tail).

Fill the head with a ribbon across the neck or even a bow. Stitch it to suit the thread

Lamb

Material

Crochet hook of 3.5mm for main body

Crochet hook of 3.25mm that will be used for bow

Cream color loops & threads shiny yarn ball

Yarn less than 200g skein of millennial color

Yarn of category 4 in soft green color for bows

Safety eyes of 12 mm size

Black color crochet thread for eyebrows and for the lips

Stuffing

Tapestry needle

Pattern

Front Body Panel: for front body panel start with crochet of 3.5mm and pink yarn

Row 1: Ch 15, starting in second ch from hook, single crochet across (14 stitchs), ch 2, turn.

Row 2: Bobble stitch, ch 1 (counts as a stitch), 2single crochet in next stitch, [Bobble stitch, single crochet] x 5, Bobble stitch, ch 1 (counts as a stitch), 2single crochet in last stitch (18 stitches), ch 1, turn.

Row 3: 2single crochet in each of the next 2 stitches, single crochet 14, 2single crochet in each of the last 2 stitches (22 stitches), ch 2, turn.

Row 4: Bobble stitch, ch 1 (counts as a stitch), single crochet, [Bobble stitch, single crochet] x 9, Bobble stitch, 2single crochet in last stitch (24 stitches), ch 1, turn.

Row 5: Single crochet 24 (24 stitches), ch 2, turn.

Row 6: [Bobble stitch, single crochet], repeat [ ] across (24 stitches), ch 1, turn.

Rows 7-12: Repeat rows 5 and 6

Row 13: Single crochet 24 (24 stitches), ch 2, turn.

In the next row, we will start the color-work for the face.

Row 14: In pink Bobble decrease, single crochet, [Bobble stitch, single crochet] x 2, in cream single crochet 10, in pink [Bobble stitch, single crochet] x 2, Bobble stitch, Single crochet 2 together. Work a regular single crochet decrease. (22 stitches), ch 1, turn.

Row 15: In pink single crochet 5, in cream single crochet 12, in pink single crochet 5 (22 stitches), ch 2, turn.

Row 16: In pink [Bobble stitch, single crochet] x 2, in cream single crochet 14, in pink [Bobble stitch, single crochet] x 2 (22 stitches), ch 1, turn.

Row 17: In pink single crochet 3, in cream single crochet 16, in pink single crochet 3 (22 stitches), ch 2, turn.

Row 18: In pink Bobble decrease, single crochet, in cream single crochet 16, in pink Bobble stitch, Single crochet 2 together. Work a regular single crochet decrease. (20 stitches), ch 1, turn.

Row 19: In pink single crochet 2, in cream single crochet 16, in pink single crochet 2 (20 stitches), ch 2, turn.

Row 20: In pink Bobble stitch, single crochet, in cream single crochet 16, in pink Bobble stitch, single crochet (20 stitches), ch 1, turn.

Row 21: In pink single crochet 3, in cream single crochet 14, in pink single crochet 3 (20 stitches), ch 2, turn.

Row 22: In pink [Bobble stitch, single crochet] x 2, in cream single crochet 12, in pink [Bobble stitch, single crochet] x 2 (20 stitches), ch 1, turn.

All remaining rows are worked in pink.

Row 23: Single crochet 2 together. Work a regular single crochet decrease., single crochet 16, Single crochet 2 together. Work a regular single crochet decrease. (18 stitches), ch 2, turn.

Row 24: [Bobble stitch, single crochet], repeat [ ] across (18 stitches), ch 1, turn.

Row 25: Single crochet 18 (18 stitches), ch 2, turn.

Row 26: Bobble stitch, Single crochet 2 together. Work a regular single crochet decrease., [Bobble stitch, single crochet] x 6, Bobble stitch, Single crochet 2 together. Work a regular single crochet decrease. (16 stitches), ch 1, turn.

Row 27: Single crochet 2 together. Work a regular single crochet decrease., single crochet 12, Single crochet 2 together. Work a regular single crochet decrease. (14 stitches), ch 2, turn

Row 28: Bobble decrease, Single crochet 2 together. Work a regular single crochet decrease., [Bobble stitch, single crochet] x 3, Bobble decrease, Single crochet 2 together. Work a regular single crochet decrease. (10 stitches)

Tie off.

Back Body Panel:

Using Pink color yarn

Rows 1-13: Repeat rows 1-13 of the front panel

Row 14: Bobble decrease, single crochet, [Bobble stitch, single crochet] x 9, Bobble stitch, Single crochet 2 together. Work a regular single crochet decrease. (22 stitches), ch 1, turn.

Row 15: Single crochet 22 (22 stitches), ch 2, turn.

Row 16: [Bobble stitch, single crochet], repeat [ ] across (22 stitches), ch 1, turn.

Row 17: Single crochet 22 (22 stitches), ch 2, turn.

Row 18: Bobble decrease, single crochet, [Bobble stitch, single crochet] x 8, Bobble stitch, Single crochet 2 together. Work a regular single crochet decrease. (20 stitches), ch 1, turn.

Row 19: Single crochet 20 (20 stitches), ch 2, turn.

Row 20: [Bobble stitch, single crochet], repeat [ ] across (20 stitches), ch 1, turn.

Row 21: Single crochet 20 (20 stitches), ch 2, turn

Row 22: [Bobble stitch, single crochet], repeat [ ] across (20 stitches), ch 1, turn

Rows 23-28: Repeat rows 23-28 of front panel.

Tie off. Set panels aside for assembly later.

Outside Ears:

Using crochet hook of 3.25mm hook and pink color yarn.

Row 1: Ch 3, starting 2nd ch from hook, single crochet 2 (2 stitches), ch 2, turn

Row 2: *(Bobble stitch, single crochet) into the same stitch*, repeat * in next stitch (4 stitches), ch 1, turn

Row 3: 2single crochet into firs stitch, single crochet 2, 2single crochet in last stitch (6 stitches), ch 2, turn

Row 4: Bobble stitch, ch 1 (counts as stitch), single crochet, Bobble stitch, single crochet, Bobble stitch, ch 1 (counts as stitch), single crochet (8 stitches), ch 1, turn

Row 5: Single crochet 8 (8 stitches), ch 2, turn

Row 6: [Bobble stitch, single crochet], repeat [ ] across (8 stitches), ch 1, turn

Row 7: Single crochet 2 together. Work a regular single crochet decrease., single crochet 4, Single crochet 2 together. Work a regular single crochet decrease. (6 stitches), ch 2, turn

Row 8: [Bobble stitch, single crochet], repeat [ ] across (6 stitches), ch 1, turn

Row 9: Single crochet 2 together. Work a regular single crochet decrease., single crochet 2, Single crochet 2 together. Work a regular single crochet decrease. (4 stitches), ch 2, turn

Row 10: [Bobble stitch, single crochet], repeat [ ] across (4 stitches), ch 1, turn

Row 11: Single crochet 2 together. Work a regular single crochet decrease. twice (2 stitches), ch 2, turn

Row 12: Bobble stitch, single crochet (2 stitches)

Tie off and weave in ends. Repeat rows 1-12 for second ear. Set aside for assembly later.

Inside Ears:

Using 3.25mm crochet hook and cream color yarn held double. Ch 1 and turn at the end of each row.

Row 1: Ch 3, starting in 2nd ch from hook, single crochet 2 (2 stitches)

Row 2: 2single crochet in each stitch (4 stitches)

Row 3: 2single crochet in first stitch, single crochet 2, 2single crochet in last stitch (6 stitches)

Row 4: 2single crochet in first stitch, single crochet 4, 2single crochet in last stitch (8 stitches)

Rows 5-6: Single crochet across (8 stitches)

Row 7: Single crochet 2 together. Work a regular single crochet decrease., single crochet 4, Single crochet 2 together. Work a regular single crochet decrease. (6 stitches)

Row 8: Single crochet across (6 stitches)

Row 9: Single crochet 2 together. Work a regular single crochet decrease., single crochet 2, Single crochet 2 together. Work a regular single crochet decrease. (4 stitches)

Row 10: Single crochet across (4 stitches)

Row 11: Single crochet 2 together. Work a regular single crochet decrease. twice (2 stitches)

Row 12: Single crochet across (2 stitches)

Tie off and weave in ends. Repeat rows 1-12 for the second ear.

Hooves:

Using a 3.5mm crochet hook and cream color yarn that is held single.

Rnd 1: MAGIC RING 4 single crochet (4 stitches)

Rnd 2: [Single crochet in first stitch, 2single crochet in next], repeat [ ] once more (6 stitches)

Rnd 3: [Single crochet 2, 2single crochet in next stitch], repeat [ ] once more (8 stitches)

Rnd 4: Single crochet around (8 stitches)

Tie off, so that long yarn tail could be used for stitching later

Reiterate rows 1 to 4 3 more times for four hooves as whole. Put it aside for assembly later.

Bow:

Using 3.25mm crotchet hook and worsted weight yarn of color as you like. Ch 1 and turn at the end of each row.

Row 1: Ch 4, starting in second ch from hook, single crochet across (3 stitches)

Rows 2-3: Single crochet across (3 stitches)

Row 4: Sc3tog (1 stitch)

Row 5: Single crochet 1 (1 stitch)

Row 6: 3single crochet into same stitch (3 stitches)

Rows 7-9: Single crochet across (3 stitches)

Tie off. Reiterate rows 1-9 for other panel. Position all panels as well as crochet around each other. Stuff out gently on either side as you crochet across. Slip stitch close to start stitch. Tie off in the ends and thread.

Cutting a yarn length in the very same color, and firmly loop around the middle. Knead a knot to tie, keeping long yarn tails for future stitches.

Reiterate the above process for the second bow.

Assembly

Step 1: Face and Hooves

Below are the parts you must have on this phase now

Now, we have to mount our features at the front panel. Attach 12 mm safety eyes to left and right sides of a face in the front panel approximately 3 or 4 stitching. The eyes will be in the 5th row, numbering up from the bottom of that same face.

Then, sew two little eyebrows over ach eye utilizing black crochet thread. Sew a 'V' for both the nose utilizing black crochet thread, also a little mouth under the nose. Eventually, straighten the hooves in such a way that they become small triangles. Sew two hooves beneath the nose on to the second full line of bobbles. Put one out from the left and right sides of the body on both the 3rd bobble. Stitch them so that the triangle points point to one another, and slightly against each other. Sew that other two hooves on either part of the bobbles 'bottom row onto the row's first bobble. This time, put the triangles in such a way that somehow the points face one another up as well as off.

Step 2: Body and Ears

Cut out two pieces of roughly 30cm/12" length pink thread each and put them aside for later. Position the two body panels around each other, trying to match both sides. Due to the additional bobbles, its back body panel will also be slightly larger / bigger than the front panel. It's common! You may try to extend the front panel mildly if you want to assist the panels align a little better, but you don't need to. As long as you make sure the bobble rows line up as you crochet around, this will function perfectly.

Getting started from the left side, as shown at top of the head, start connecting both panels together by simply crocheting across the panels outdoors pink. Take a couple stitches along your head and stop until you hit the middle of your nose.

Now we're having the first ear attached. Place the ear between the doors. The ear should be placed in such a way that it faces downwards and somewhat forward so you see some of the cream color within the ear. Knit the ear into position between panels by stitching into all three pieces, the front panel, the ear and the rear panel with such a length of yarn that you put aside previously using your tapestry needle. As the ear is very thick, to keep it safe, you may need to stitch through several times. When done, tie a knot between the body panels to protect and cover the yarn tails.

Begin to crochet head and body downwards. After reaching the ear, you can single crochet in front panel stitches only (because this segment is already stitched shut). When past the ear start to crochet all panels together as usual. Keep on crocheting about. When you hit the another side of your body, stop until you get to the center of your nose.

Now stuff the body. Connect the second ear when usually crammed the very same way that you did for the first. Keep on crocheting throughout. Stuffing on top when you go. The stuffing must be extremely solid. Start crocheting over the head row. when you're totally satisfied with stuffing, slip stitch to beginning stitch to close. Inner woven yarn neck. Sew the bows across each ear to the top. Complete the part with such a carving needle for both the eyes and you will be done! (Hewitt)

Conclusion

Learning to crochet is a skill you will find useful because you can take what you learn and turn it into garments and projects that provide joy and utility for people who use them. There is a large variety of uses for the crochet stitches covered in this book. With your imagination, you can take your new knowledge of the stitches and create your own patterns and designs to make a variety of projects of your own.

Keep your hands relaxed so that you are not tensing up and tiring your fingers and hands. By relaxing, your stitches will come freely, and by practicing, you will be able to unravel the stitches that don't measure up to your standard, retry the stitches over and over again.

Take the stitches you have learned and make swatches of the stitches. This practice will pay off handsomely as you perfect the stitches and grow comfortable handling crochet hooks of different sizes. Practicing is the best way to feel good about your skills. You will be able to see how much easier the stitches are made when you are familiar with how the yarn feels in your hands and how it moves along the crochet hook. This book takes away the intimidating features of crochet. Make the projects in the book and you'll see why people enjoy crochet and all that it has to offer. Relax and enjoy using what you learn to produce actual items that you can use and enjoy.

So what are you waiting for? Grab that hook and pick out your favorite color of yarn, and start your brand new hobby now!

BOOK 2 :
CROCHET FOR BEGINNERS ADVANCED GUIDE

THE COMPLETE STEP BY STEP GUIDE TO LEARN ADVANCED STITCHES AND PATTERNS WITH ILLUSTRATIONS AND TIPS TO CREATE YOUR PROJECTS IN COMPLETE AUTONOMY

PATTY WILSON

Introduction

This book takes away the intimidating features of crochet. The language of crochet is defined, and the patterns are explained in plain English. Join the crochet community by putting your new skills into action. Make the projects in the book and you'll see why people enjoy crochet and all that it has to offer. Relax and enjoy using what you learn to produce actual items that you can use and enjoy.

The author of this eye-opening book aims to share her knowledge and passion on the subject and help more and more people to learn crochet in a simple and fast way so you can play in complete autonomy this extraordinary hobby. This is a complete guide to Crocheting and in this book, you will find modern crochet projects as you know crochet is increasingly fashionable and even designers have garments made with crochet in their parades. This guide on crochet for beginners explains the basics of how to crochet (tools, materials, terms, and abbreviations). It includes the basic techniques and stitches specifically for beginners and easy and quick patterns for beginners.

Keep your hands relaxed so that you are not tensing up and tiring your fingers and hands. By relaxing, your stitches will come freely, and by practicing, you will be able to unravel the stitches that don't measure up to your standard, retry the stitches over and over again. You will find that you like some stitches more than others. By mastering the basic stitches, you will be able to tolerate your least favorites. The first row is always the most grueling.

Make sure your foundation chain is even and not too tight. This will make it easier to fit the hook into the chain when you are making the first row of stitches.

You will relay your skills to those around you once you learn to crochet. Many families exchange crochet pieces from one generation to the next. Crochet heirlooms may be a symbol of the heritage of pride and love.

Crochet is also remarkably easier to pick up over knitting; crochet has very simple beginner stitches that you can use even in the early stages of learning to create cute and funky little objects. It is a great encouragement for a beginner to see their hard work begin to grow and take shape in front of them.

Chapter 1: Advanced Stitches

Picot Stitch

If you may recall, picot stitches are used to work on the edges of finished items. They're also used to make detailed, beautiful stitches, and could also be turned into squares.

1. Make sure that you work exactly on the edge of a finished stitch.

2. Then, start single crocheting in the first stitch before crocheting in the next stitch, which would then be the third chain.

3. Then, go on and make more single crochets in the next 3 stitches to make the picot. Check it out below.

4. Then, repeat step 3 all across the row.

Moss Stitch

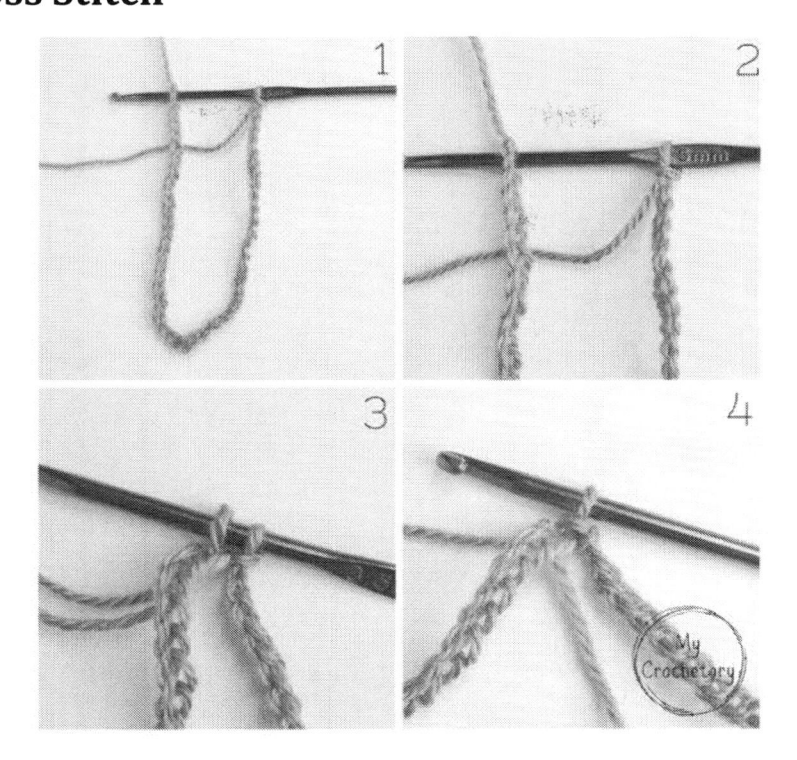

1. **Row 1:** Create a chain of stitches that are even in number. Sc in the fourth chain from your hook, **ch 1, sk 1 chain, sc in the chain that follows**, rework to the end. Chain 2, turn.
2. **Row 2:** sc in the following chain space, **ch 1 sc in chain space that follows,** rework up to the end completing with sc in the chain space from the row before.
3. Continue to work the second row till you achieve your preferred length.

Textured Crochet Stitch

Create a chain with even stitches.

1. **Round 1:** sc 2 chains together in the second and third chain from the hook, **ch 1, sc 2 chains together over the 2 chains that follow; rework from *** to the final chain, ch 1, sc in the final chain.
2. **Round 2:** ch 1, turn, sc 2 chains together over the first stitch and chain 1 space, **ch 1, sc 2 chains together over the first stitch and chain 1 space; rework from *** to the final st, ch 1, sc in the final stitch.
3. Rework the second row until your work reaches your desired length.

Checkerboard Stitch

The Checkerboard Stitch is one of the neatest stitches out there. It's meant to crochet or dishcloth squares together and is usually used to create Afghans and the like.

1. First, you have to start with a chain. From the 3rd stitch on your hook, make a double crochet stitch and repeat this on the next stitch as well.

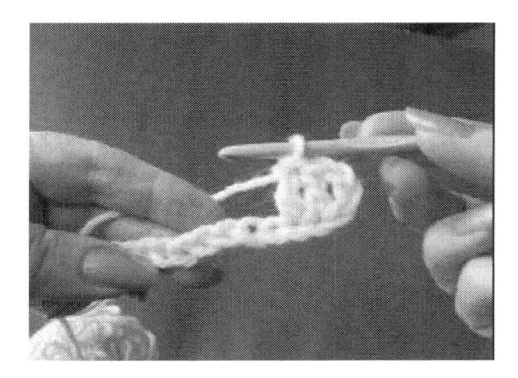

2. Then, create chain 3, and make sure to skip the next 3 stitches. Once you have done so, double crochet until the next 3 stitches.

3. Repeat the given steps above until you reach the end of your row. Make sure to end the last stitch with a double crochet.

4. Next, make a chain 3 and then turn your work over. Then, make 2 double crochet stitches in the previous row's chain 3.

5. Next, you have to make another chain 3 and make sure to double crochet right in the space of the second row, where you have not made anything earlier.

6. Make sure to repeat all the steps towards the next row, and keep doing so until you reach your desired size and shape.

Popcorn Stitch

This stitch is named as such because it does look like one. A popcorn stitch is a rounded and compact stitch that pops out. You can place your popcorn stitch in front or back—it all depends on the effect you want to achieve in your piece.

1. In making a popcorn stitch, you need 5 dc together in one stitch.

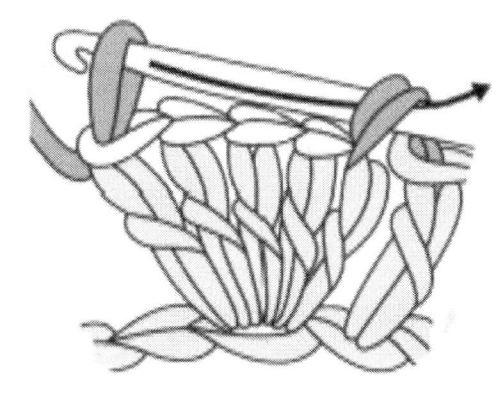

2. Remove your hook from your current loop; make sure not to lose the current loop and just drop it in the meantime.
3. Insert your hook in front (as shown) of the first dc in the group if you want to pop your stitch in front. Insert your hook from the back if you want it to pop at the back.
4. Hook your dropped loop and let it slip through the dc stitch to get a popcorn stitch.

V-Stitches

V-stitches resemble the letter V, hence the name. You can crochet loosely using this stitch, especially if you want to create lacy designs. You can also make your stitches tight and compressed.

1. To begin, do a dc, ch 1, and another dc on the same stitch. In between the two stitches, the single ch st separates the two dcs (to resemble the letter "V"). Keep in mind that the two dcs should be on the same stitch.

Puff Stitch

The puff stitches create a different texture to your work. This stitch follows the same procedure as the cluster, but you need to place all the dc stitches in the same stitch. You also need to work on 3 dc stitches to create one puff stitch.

1. To start, make a dc stitch and leave the last two loops open or hanging. You should have one unfinished dc stitch on your hook.

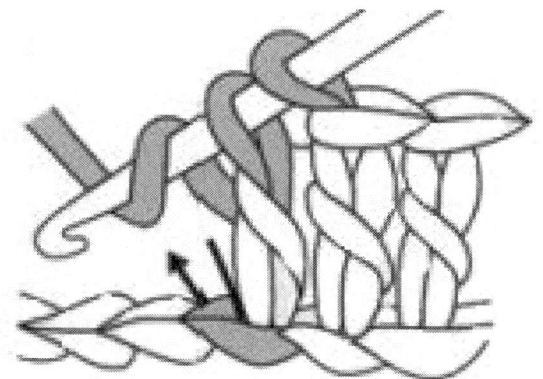

2. Start with your second dc stitch on the same stitch as the first unfinished dc. Leave the three loops hanging from your hook.

3. Now, begin your third and last dc for your puff stitch and bring it together with the first two dc stitches on the same spot. Yarn over, then slip the thread through the first two loops, and you will have four loops hanging on your hook. Yarn over, then slip the thread through the four remaining loops and you will get a dc puff stitch.

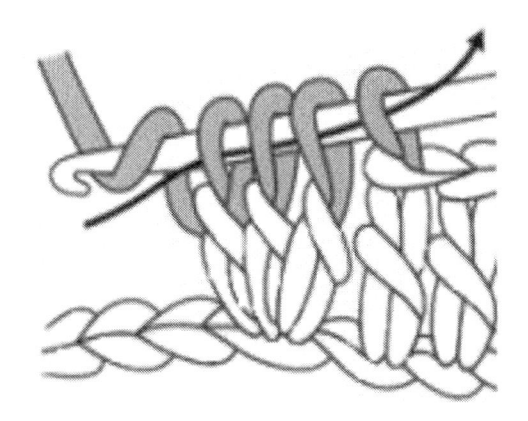

Cable Stitch

1. Start by chaining multiples of 4 stitches, then add 3 more. 16 stitches are equal to 4 cables. From the second row of the hook, go on and make single stitches. Do this for each part of the chain.

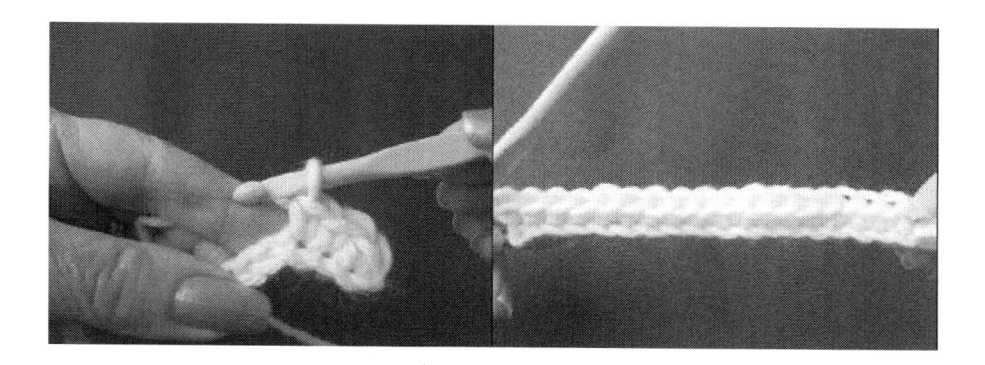

2. Next, make chain 3 and then turn your work before skipping the next stitch. Work on the next 3 stitches by double-crocheting.

3. Work from front to back by inserting your hook, and do it into the first stitch that you have skipped.

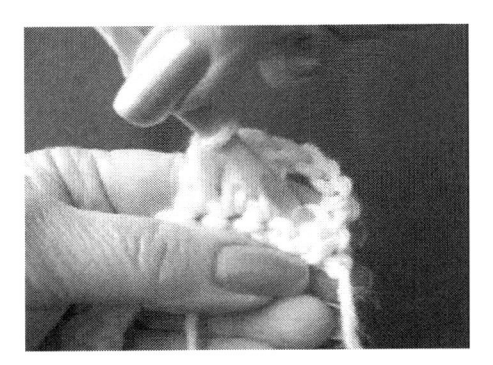

4. Then, loosely draw a loop and take it to the top of the last stitch that you have worked on. Do a yarn over to finish the stitch, and make sure it goes all the way through the loops.

5. Repeat steps 1 to 4 all across the row, then end with double crochet before chaining 1 and make a single crochet.

6. Repeat all the given steps once more to create something that resembles the one below:

Cluster Stitch

The cluster stitch is made up of a number of stitches that are half-closed, then joined together as described below.

1. Make a slip knot and create your foundation chain.
2. Yarn over hook, insert the hook into the next stitch.

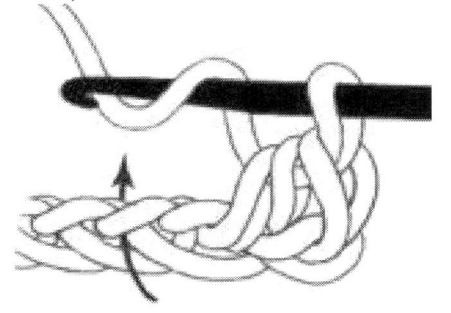

3. Yarn over, draw yarn through the stitch.
4. Yarn over, draw through 2 loops on the hook.

5. Repeat steps 2 to 4 three times.
6. Yarn over and draw through the 5 loops on the hook. This completes a cluster created with 4 double crochet stitches.

Basketweave Stitch

One of the most interesting types of stitches out there, the Basketweave Stitch basically looks like a basket. Sometimes, it's also known as the Waffle Stitch. You'd use a lot of single and double crochet stitches here.

1. Make chain 22, or a foundation piece where you could then work on the rest of your stitches to complete the basketweave stitch.

2. From the 3rd stitch from the hook, start making double crochet stitches. Do this into each stitch of the chain.

3. Chain 2 and turn to make the front post stitch, and then yarn over and insert your hook over the previous row's double crochet stitches.

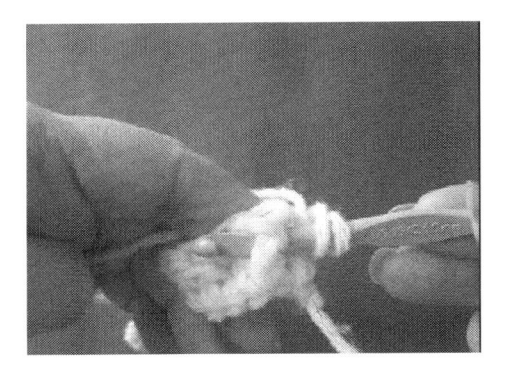

4. Repeat the process in the next 2 stitches that you're going to make so that you'd get a total of 4 front post stitches.

5. Then, do the back stitch post by inserting the hook behind the previous row's double crochet stitches, and then go and complete a double crochet.

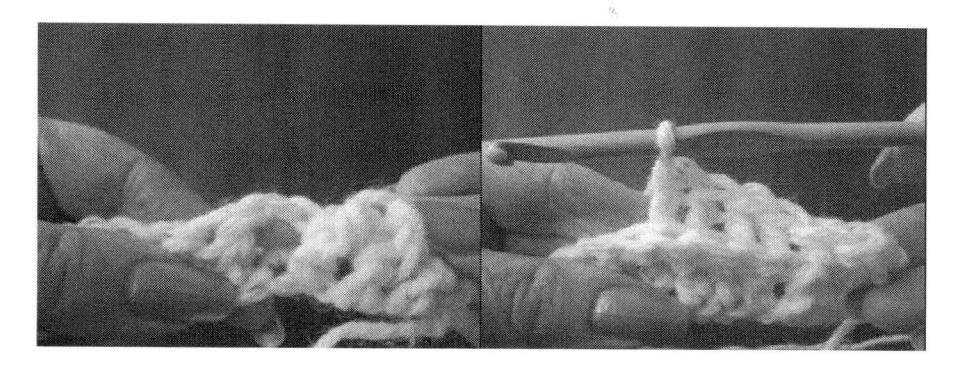

6. Continue doing as you're told, and then when you see that you have reached the end of the row, make a chain 2, and then turn, and repeat making your double crochet stitches.

7. Whatever you have done on your earlier row, that's also what you have to do in the next row (i.e., 4 stitches = 4 stitches). Continue doing so until you create the length of fabric you want.

Moss Stitch

This stitch is also known as granite stitch. It is very easy to do, as it requires you to know only the chain stitch and the single crochet stitch.

1. To begin, you will need to crochet an odd number of chain stitches. You can place a marker in the first chain stitch from the hook, just to keep track of where you need to work your stitches. Once you get the hang of it, you can stop using the marker. So, having placed the marker, you can continue with the work. You will crochet an sc stitch into the third chain from the hook.

2. Chain one and turn your work. In the second row, you will work sc stitches into each chain one space and separate them by chain one. You will repeat this until the end of the row, where you will work an sc stitch into the chain stitch where you have placed the marker, removing it before crocheting the stitch.

Seed Stitch

Seed Stitches are series of alternating double and single crochet stitches, which would then give you a result of a closed stitch.

1. First, you have to start with a chain. Then, make a turn and start single crocheting from the 2nd stitch you see on the hook.

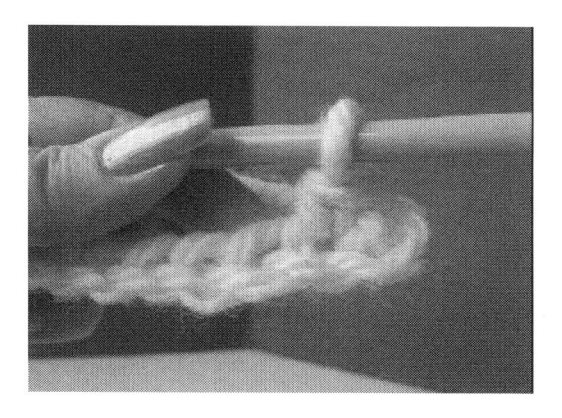

2. Now, the next thing you have to do for the next stitch is to make a double crochet.

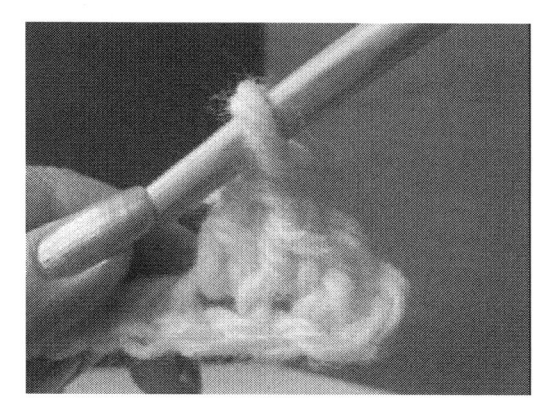

3. Then, for the next stitch, you have to single crochet.

4. Across the row, all you'd have to do is repeat steps 2 and 3, to create a row of complete seed stitches.

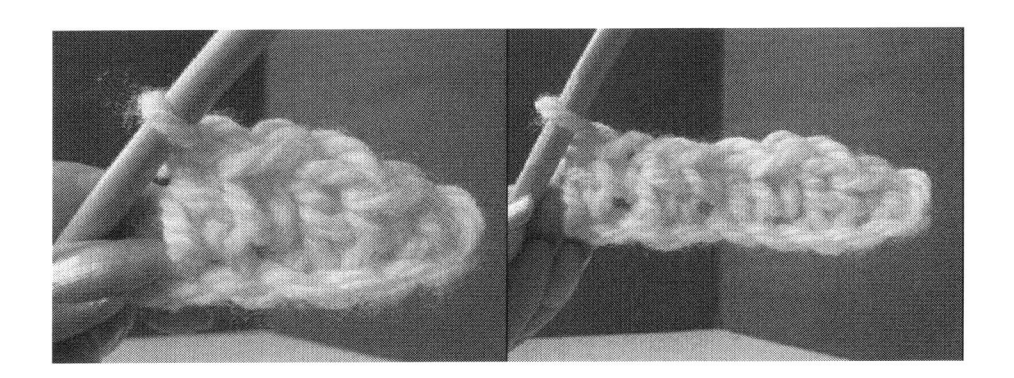

5. Now, once you reach the end of the row, it's time for you to turn in what you're working on. If it ends on a single stitch, do a double stitch next, and vice versa.

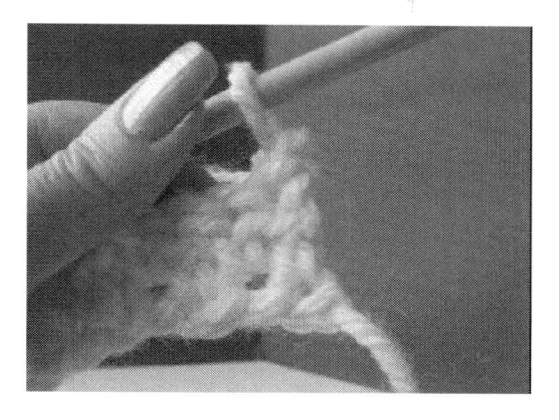

6. Make sure that you work your way through the row. Just repeat steps 2 to 3 until you reach your desired length and texture.

Shell Stitch

1. To create the shell stitch, you will make multiple chains of six stitches, or if you want to use the stitch as an edging, you will count in sixes for the number of shells you will make, and you will add one more chain. The first two chains from the hook will count as one double crochet (dc). Then, you will work five dc into the third chain.

2. The set of five dc creates the shell effect. To secure the first shell, you will skip two chain stitches and work a single crochet (sc) into the chain stitch afterward. So, to complete the row, you will repeat the following: skip two stitches, work five dc into the third stitch, skip two stitches, and work a sc into the sixth stitch. You will repeat this until the end of the row, ending with a sc. If you work only one row of sc, it will make a wonderful edging, but you can also work in multiple rows and create something bigger, like a blanket or a pillowcase.

Surface Slip Stitch

1. Start with a field of crochet stitches; this example is single crochet.
2. Insert your hook from top to bottom through the work you'd like to start the surface crochet stitches.
3. From the bottom, take the yarn for the surface crochet, make a loop over the crochet hook, and gently pull through the work.
4. Pull through a loop from the yarn's working end, and then pull through the work like a slip stitch through the other loop.
5. Continue in the desired pattern.

Chapter 2: Crochet for both English and American

American or UK / International Crochet Terminology

There are two very similar but different ways to write crochet instructions. Both approaches are generally referred to as American Crochet and UK / International Crochet Terminology. Looking at the lists below, you can see that the UK / International words list has no single crochet. It results in the names of the stitches being moved out of alignment.

AMERICAN	UK/INTERNATIONAL
(ch) - Chain	(ch) - Chain
(sl st) - Slip Stitch	(sl st) - Slip Stitch
(sc) Single Crochet	(dc) - Double Crochet
(dc) Double Crochet	(tr) - Treble Crochet
(hdc) - Half Double Crochet	(htr) - Half Treble Crochet

But how do I know which terminology was used?

The question of which jargon is used is essentially the same as the question of where the pattern was written. It is almost likely that American crochet language would have been used if this was an American publication.

Models released in the United Kingdom and Australia will continue to use UK / International Terminology. Find out if the pattern was written anywhere in one of these countries.

While UK / International Terminology is the worldwide standard, some countries prefer to use American crochet terminology for internet control.

Commercially printed designs should have the address of the printer, and the country of origin will most often be written on it. Most publishers have websites; search the address or phone number, this will give you a description of the company's nationality.

When you cannot locate an address or a telephone number, send them an e-mail.

When you start making a lot of patterns, you become acquainted with the big publishers and know the language they use. There is an increasing trend for online pattern publishers to choose which terminology you would like. Not all patterns will tell you where the pattern was written. Your detective skills come into play here!

Here Are Some Suggestions and Strategies for Deciding

Can You See the Words Single Crochet or Sc in the Pattern?

Single crochet is not part of the UK / International crochet pattern vocabulary, and it does not appear on a UK-published design. You may conclude that the pattern was written using the American crochet language if you see it in the book.

Even a half triple of US crochet terminology is uncommon, but if you see it, you should presume that they have written directions using the UK / International crochet terminology unless something else is indicated.

Some designs come with a stitch guide. Unless the stitch is not made as you think it should be, it has possibly been written in the 'other' language of the crochet.

Do You Look at the Image?

After a little practice, you start identifying the stitches in photographs, etc. You can be sure of the usage of UK / International crochet jargon when you understand the stitch as a single crochet in the picture and it says you do a double crochet (DC).

Furthermore, you recognize that a double crochet stitch is being used, and the template reads single crochet terms (sc).

How Do You Know the Name of a Yarn?

Various yarn weights have different names depending on the country in which they were produced. Double knitting yarn is the same as worsted American and Australian weight yarn. It is unusual to use yarn from another country for a pattern creator. The yarn style and brand give you an idea of the pattern and show the terms used.

Hook Type Used

America has its own alphabetical hook sizing system as well as metric (mm) measurements. If the pattern calls for an H or J knot, begin to believe the pattern may come from America Crochet Conditions—Americans use the word 'gage' for stress and miss.

The American Craft Yarn Council acknowledges skill levels from the novice to the seasoned. American patterns also have the ability level emblem of the Yarn Council, which you do not often see on the UK or international patterns.

That being said, is the tension square the correct size, and does it look the same as in the picture?

If it looks wrong and it is the wrong size, you are probably using the wrong stitch, is this due to the pattern using another crochet terminology? It may be!

You will now have a clear understanding of the words your design uses. If you still cannot work it out, consider asking for assistance at your nearest wool shop or an internet site.

Some of the crochet patterns that you could find could be American, but others might be from anywhere else around the world. Some countries use other crochet words that vary elsewhere.

For example, American and British patterns differ in a variety of crochet words. The key differences are significant because if the opposite interpretation is used, they may alter a pattern entirely.

In Britain, the American slip-stitch crochet technique is referred to as a single crochet. An American single crochet is a double crochet in Britain. Similarly, an American double hook is called a single crochet, and a British double crochet is an American single crochet.

It is necessary to understand exactly what country words are used by people who know how to crochet and use various patterns. Using American terms in a British template may cause damage to the project and vice versa.

Most patterns should show where they come from. The terms used for crochets should not be too complicated as long as care is taken.

The Difference between American and British Crochet Terms

American and British crochet terms differ slightly, and this can be very confusing to the beginner. The first thing you need to do is to determine if your pattern is written using the American method or the British method. Sometimes this is as easy as looking at where a magazine was published. I have created a chart below to show you the differences. The stitches are the same, but they have different names as you will see.

In this little book, we will be using the American system for crochet stitches. It is a pity that the two systems have not been merged into one, but perhaps one day they will be.

Until then, if you are uncertain, you can always ask at your local yarn shop, they should be able to tell you which system is being used in your pattern by looking at a photograph of the object to be crocheted or the chart being used in the pattern if there is one.

Crochet Abbreviations

Crochet Abbreviations

Use this chart to convert UK crochet terms to US terms when needed.

UK		US	
Chain	Ch	Chain	Ch
Slip Stitch	Ss	Slip Stitch	Ss
Double Crochet	Dc	Single Crochet	Sc
Half Treble	Htr	Half Double	hdc
Treble	Tr	Double	Dc
Double Treble	dtr	Treble	Tr
Triple Treble	ttr	Double Treble	dtr

Now that we have chosen a crochet hook, some yarn, and have decided to work with the American crochet terms, we are ready to begin.

If you knit within the American or United Kingdom style, keep the yarn in the middle of your fingers, as well as wrap it freely around the needle to make the bind off stitch without drawing it as tight as you would with a typical knit or purl stitch.

Most significantly, inspect the tension after the last bind-off stitch as well as before you reduced the yarn. If it also looks tight, meticulously unpick the stitches, putting the stitches back on a needle, and redo the bind off. Yes, I've done this too.

How to Read Stitch Patterns for both English and American?

You'll find stitch patterns written in two different ways. The first is the most typical, and you will find it in vintage patterns, as well as many modern American and British patterns. This is a fully written out stitch pattern, using typical and traditional stitch notation. Below, you'll find a list of common abbreviations, and a few notes about translation issues, as well as a sample pattern and a breakdown of what it means. Some modern designers in the west, as well as Japanese crochet patterns, do not rely upon written out notation, but on a graphic representation of crochet stitches. These look nothing at all like craft charts you might have used, like those for cross-stitching or knitting. They are, in fact, rather pictorial, with picture symbols written out for each round or row. Once you're used to reading crochet charts, you'll find you can do so with relative ease.

- Charts are much more commonly used for doilies or shawls, rather than simple projects, like a hat or afghan.

- Charts are rarely used for repeated stitch patterns but can be.

Written crochet patterns are still the most common in America and Britain. They are relatively easy to use, and pattern notation is largely standardized.

Common Abbreviations

approx	approximately
beg	beginning
blo	back loop only
cc	contrast color
ch	chain
cl	cluster
cont	continue
dc	double crochet
dec	decrease
ea	each
gm	grams
gr	group
hdc	half double crochet
hk	hook
inc	increase
incl	including
lp	loop

mc	main color
pat	pattern
rem	remaining
rep	repeat
rnd(s)	round(s)
RS	right side
sc	single crochet
sl	slip
slst	slip stitch
sk	skip
sp	space
st(s)	stitch(es)
tog	together
tr / tc	triple (treble) crochet
WS	wrong side
yo	yarn over

Which of these are the most common? For crochets, they're fairly simple: yo, ch, sc, hdc, dc, tc. Nearly all crochet patterns are made up of these basic stitches, put together in different ways. Most patterns also include a key explaining specific abbreviations. You may find this especially helpful if the pattern includes particular stitch patterns or combinations or if you've not crocheted for some time.

Let's look at a simple shell stitch pattern. This pattern can be used for a variety of different projects, making a pretty and feminine garment or blanket. It's relatively quick to work and is easily memorized.

Make a chain of the desired length, plus 3 stitches for turning.

Row 1: Make 5 dc in the 3rd st from the end, skip 2 ch, make 1 sc in next stitch, skip 2 and make 5 dc in next stitch.

Row 2: Ch 3, and turn. Work 4 dc into sc. 1 sc into 3rd dc of the previous row, 5 dc into sc of previous row. Repeat from * across row.

Repeat row 2 to the desired length.

Let's take a longer look at this in a written-out form:

Row 1: Make 5 double crochet stitches in the third stitch from the end of the chain. Skip 2 chains, make one single crochet in the next stitch, skip 2 chains and make 5 double crochet stitches in the next stitch.

Row 2: Chain 3 and turn. Work 4 double crochet into single crochet. Work one single crochet into 3rd double crochet of the previous row, 5 double crochet into the single crochet of the previous row.

With just a little practice, the abbreviations will become second nature. You'll find them used throughout the patterns in this book.

Note: If you're an American and use a British pattern or you're British and use an American pattern, there's a bit of a quirk between the two languages.

British Notation	American Notation
double crochet (dc)	single crochet (sc)
half treble (htr)	half double crochet (hdc)
treble (tr)	double crochet (dc)
double treble (dtr)	treble (tr)
triple treble (trtr)	double treble (dtr)
miss	skip
tension	gauge
yarn over hook (yoh)	yarn over (yo)

Do you see the difference? The UK doesn't use the term single crochet; a single crochet is called a double, and a double crochet is called a treble. The treble crochet is called a double treble. Reviewing the pattern key can help you to know whether you're working with a British or American pattern, but it's an easy adjustment, especially as you get used to working the pattern.

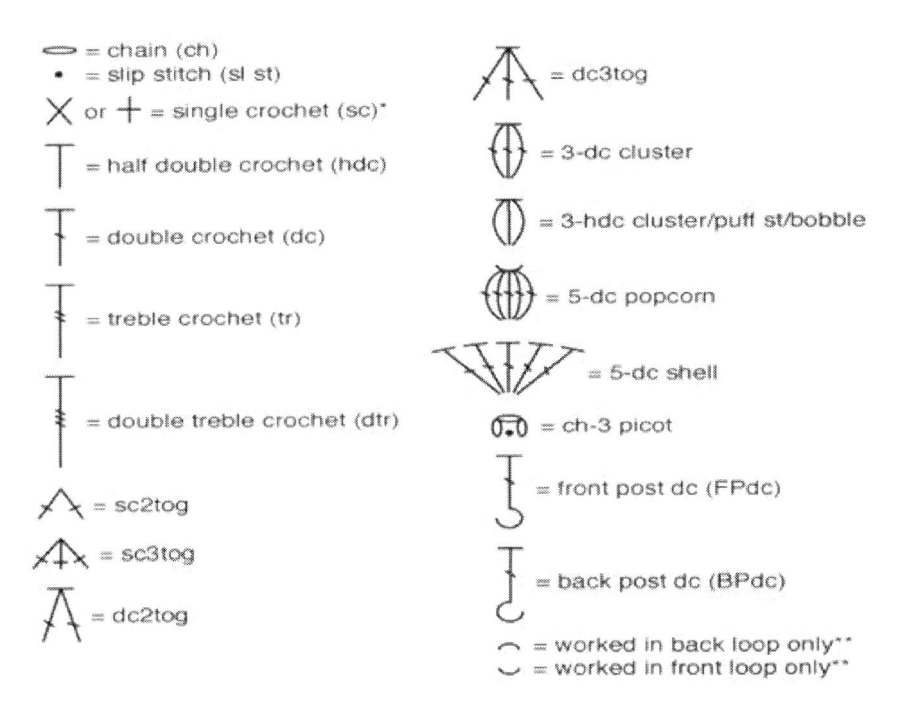

```
⌒ = chain (ch)
• = slip stitch (sl st)
X or + = single crochet (sc)*
T = half double crochet (hdc)
† = double crochet (dc)
‡ = treble crochet (tr)
‡ = double treble crochet (dtr)
⋏ = sc2tog
⋏ = sc3tog
⋏ = dc2tog

⋏ = dc3tog
⊕ = 3-dc cluster
⊕ = 3-hdc cluster/puff st/bobble
⊕ = 5-dc popcorn
⋎ = 5-dc shell
⊙ = ch-3 picot
= front post dc (FPdc)
= back post dc (BPdc)
⌢ = worked in back loop only**
⌣ = worked in front loop only**
```

* Both symbols are commonly used for single crochet
** Symbol appears at base of stitch being worked

The key above illustrates crochet chart symbols. The symbols themselves are universal but do notice that the language refers to American crochet notation and work the stitches accordingly.

When assembled to form a chart, the symbols might look like this:

You may notice something about this chart right away. It creates a visual very similar to the finished work, making it easy to realize what your project should look like, even if you don't have a picture of the finished work.

Round 1: Ch 16, join with a sl st.

Round 2: Ch 3, work one dc in the first chain of the previous round. *Work one dc in next stitch, 2 dc in next around* join with a sl st. (24)

Round 3: Ch 3, sk 1 dc, sc in next, ch 3, sk 1 dc, sc in next join with a sl st.

Round 4: Ch 3, 1 dc in first sc, sk 1 ch, 10 dc in 2nd ch stitch, sk 1 ch, 1 sc in sc* to last ch 3 loops. 9 dc in 2nd ch st, sl st to join to 3rd ch in initial ch 3.

Round 5: Sc in 6th dc of last dc cluster, ch 5, dc in sc of previous round, ch5, *sc in 6th dc of the cluster, ch 10, dc in sc of previous round, ch 5, dc in sc of previous round, ch 5* join with sl st.

Round 6: Working backward to reverse direction, slip stitch in the first 5 ch stitches to the left of your hook. This returns you to the corner of your work. Ch 8, sc in the third ch of ch 5 of the previous round. *Ch 5 sc in the third ch of ch 5 of the previous round. Ch5, dc 3 in 6th ch of ch 10 of previous round, ch 3, dc 3 in same space*. On the last repeat, dc 2, using the first 3 chains of initial chain 8 to make the third dc. Join with sl st at the third chain.

Round 7: Working backward again, sl st in the first 5 stitches to reach the corner of your work. Ch 8, sc in the third ch of ch 5 of the previous round. *Ch 5 sc in the third ch of ch 5 of the previous round. Ch 5, sc in the third ch of ch 5 of previous round, dc 3 in 6th ch of ch 10 of previous round, ch 3, dc3 in same space*. On the last repeat, dc 2, using the first 3 chains of initial chain 8 to make the third dc. Join with sl st at the third chain.

Round 8: Working backward again, sl st in the first 5 stitches to reach the corner of your work. Ch 8, sc in the third ch of ch 5 of the previous round. *Ch 5 sc in the third ch of ch 5 of the previous round. Ch5, sc in the third ch of ch 5 of previous round, Ch5, sc in the third ch of ch 5 of previous round, dc 3 in 6th ch of ch 10 of previous round, ch 3, dc3 in same space*. On the last repeat, dc 2, using the first 3 chains of initial chain 8 to make the third dc. Join with sl st at the third chain.

(**Note:** Rounds 6, 7, and 8 are nearly identical, with the addition of one more ch 5 loop per side in each round.)

As you can see, that's a very cumbersome pattern written out. It's much easier to follow and understand working from a pictorial chart. This is the benefit of charts for complex and lacy work. If you'd like, you can even make your own charts, either by hand or using online charting software.

Lightweight Textured Stitch Patterns

Textured Single Crochet

Foundation chain: multiple of 2 + 3 stitches.

Row 1: Work 1 sc in 3rd ch from hook, sk 1 ch, 2 sc into next ch, repeat from * to last 2 ch, sk 1 ch, 1 sc into the last ch, turn.

Row 2: Ch 1 (counts as first sc), 1 sc in first sc, sk 1 sc, 2 sc into next sc, repeat from * to last 2 sts to last 2 sts, sk 1 sc, 1 sc in top of the chain used to turn. Repeat row 2 to the desired length.

Crochet Seed Stitch

Foundation chain: multiple of 2 + 1.

Row 1: Sc in the second chain from hook, dc in next. Repeat to end of row.

Row 2: Ch 1, sc in the first stitch, dc in next. Repeat to end of row.

Repeat row 2 to the desired length.

Ribbed Seed Stitch

Working through the back loop creates the ribbed texture.

Foundation chain: multiple of 2 + 1.

Row 1: Sc in the back loop in 2nd ch from hook, dc in the back loop in next. Repeat to end of row.

Row 2: Ch 1, sctbl in the first stitch, dctbl in next. Repeat to end of row. Repeat row 2 to the desired length.

Waffle Stitch

Foundation row: Multiple of 4 plus 3 stitches.

Row 1: Work one row in single crochet. Ch 3, turn.

Row 2: Dc in next, ch 2, sk 2 sts, dc in next 2 sts. Repeat from * across. Ch 3, turn.

Row 3: Dc in next dc. 1 tr in each of the next 2 sk sts, working each treble behind the ch2 of the previous row. Dc in next 2. Repeat from * across. Ch 3, turn.

Repeat rows 2 and 3 to the desired length.

Waffle Stitch Variation

This stitch works particularly well in hand-dyed or mixed yarns.

Row 1: Ch 23. Sc in the second ch from hook and in each chain stitch across. Ch 3, turn.

Row 2: Dc in next, ch 2, sk next 2 sts dc in next 2. Repeat from * across. End with a dc in the last 2 sts. Ch 3, turn.

Row 3: Dc in next st, tr in first sk st working in front of ch 2 space. Tr in the next skipped stitch, inserting the hook behind the ch 2 space. Dc in next 2 dc. Repeat from * across. Ch 3, turn.

Repeat rows 2 and 3 as desired.

Finish with a row beginning with ch 1, sc across.

Brick Stitch

Foundation Chain: Multiple of 4.

Row 1: Work 3 dc in the 4th chain from the hook, sk 3 chains, sc in next chain, chain 3, 3 dc in the same chain. Repeat from * across row, ending with sc.

Row 2: Work 3 chains to turn. 3 dc in sc of prev. row. Sc in next ch 3 space of previous row, chain 3, 3 dc in same ch 3 space. Repeat from * across row. End with sc in last ch 3 of the previous row.

Repeat row 2 to the needed length.

Shell Stitch

You can vary the shell stitch by replacing the double crochet stitches with either half double or treble crochet stitches; you may also work more or fewer stitches in each shell shape. You may also skip more stitches between shells for a slightly different appearance. The shell stitch is slightly lacy, producing a relatively feminine appearance.

Foundation Chain: Multiple of 6 stitches plus 1.

Row 1: Ch 1, 1 sc in 2nd chain from the hook, skip 2 chains, 5 dc in next chain, skip 2 chains, 1 sc in next ch, rep from to end of row. Turn.

Row 2: Ch 3 (counts as first dc), 2 dc in same st as ch3 just made, skip 2 dc, 1 sc in next dc (center st of the 5 dc shell), skip 2 dc, 5 dc in next sc *, repeat from * to * to end of the row, ending the last repeat with 3 dc in last sc, skip turning chain. Turn.

Row 3: Ch 1, 1 sc in first st, sk 2 dc, 5 dc in next sc, sk 2 dc, 1 sc in next dc, repeat till end of the row, to end with sc.

Repeat rows 2 and 3 to the desired length.

Wave Stitch

This stitch works best worked in three different colors, but it can be done in a single color if you prefer.

Foundation chain: Multiple of 14.

Row 1: In 3rd chain from hook, dc 3.*Sk 3 chains, sc in next 7 ch. Sk 3 ch, 7 dc in next ch.*

Row 2: Ch 1, sc across row.

Row 3: Ch 1, sc in next 4 stitches, *Sk 3 ch, 7 dc in next stitch. Sk 3, 7 sc to last Sk 3, then work 4 sc.

Row 4: Repeat row 2.

Repeat rows 1–4 to the desired length.

Chapter 3: Techniques

Joining Yarns

Even giant balls of yarn run out eventually, so learning to join a new yarn while crocheting a piece is a must for new crocheters. Joining yarn into a project is also part of the process of changing colors in crochet, so crocheters who are looking to stretch their crafting wings might be interested to learn this process as well.

There are many and diverse ways to join yarn while crocheting; two commonly used methods include gently tying the yarns together to be undone later and crocheting the new yarn into the piece. Some crocheters prefer the first method because it feels stable, while others prefer the second because it can leave less work for the finishing stage. Sometimes the project will dictate the best way to join a yarn; delicate, open projects might need the former, while chunky, closely crocheted projects will often do fine with the latter.

Tying

To join the yarn at the end of a row using the tying method, the crocheter simply finishes the row, then gently ties the two yarns together about 1 inch from the work. When the crocheter begins to crochet the new row with the new yarn, the 1 inch of old yarn will hang down while the new yarn will be snugged into the next stitch or chain. At least 6 inches of tail should be left at the end of each yarn after the knot; when the work is finished, the crocheter unties the knot, then weaves in the ends as usual.

To join the yarn in the middle of the row, the crocheter needs to first completely finish the stitch being worked. Leaving a 6-inch tail of both yarns, the crocheter knots the two yarns together, then begins the next stitch. The knot is snugged against the work so that the two stitches (old yarn and new) maintain the tension. As with joining at the end of the row, the knot needs to be untied when the project is finished so that the ends can be woven in.

Increase/Decrease

To create 'shapes' in your crochet work, you may at times need to increase or decrease the number of stitches in the row that you are working on.

Decreasing

Regardless of the actual stitch you are using, the basic technique for decreasing remains the same – you will crochet two or more stitches together to reduce them down to one stitch.

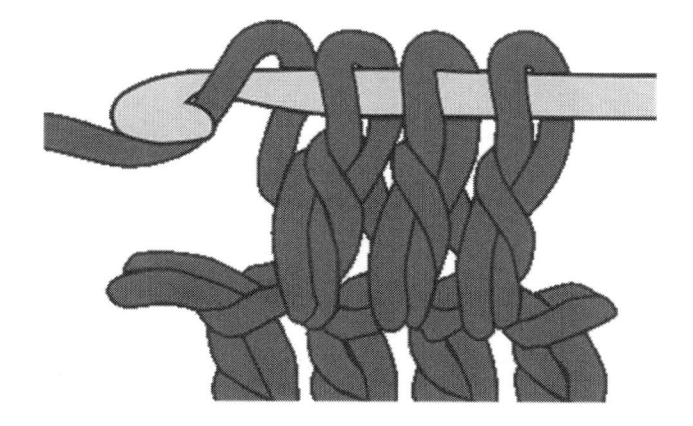

Here we wanted to work three treble stitches together (tr3tog). Work a treble stitch into each of three stitches as normal, but leave the last loop of each on the hook. You will be left with three loops on the hook. Yarn over hook (yrh), and pull through all three stitches. You will then be left with 1 loop on your hook.

Increasing

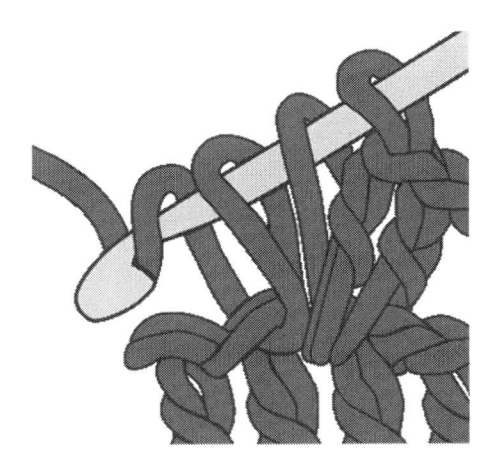

To increase your row by a stitch, you will work two or three stitches into same stitch. Here we have crocheted two stitches into the same stitch. Work one stitch as normal. Insert your hook into the stitch you have just worked and do a second stitch. You have now increased your row by one stitch.

Increase and Decrease Within A Row

For a decrease within a row, in the first step, two loops are taken from the previous row in order to remove a stitch. For the removal of two bristles, three slings from the previous series must be collected together. To increase a mesh between two vertical mesh wires of the previous row, pull a horizontal wire mesh and in the second pass, pull a sling.

Increasing on the Edge

To gain a chest on the right edge, make a loop through the edge stitch. If you want to add a stitch on the left edge, a loop is made through the horizontal edge of the edge stitch, and then the edge loop is executed. If you want to increase the number of cases at the beginning of the work, proceed as follows.

Increase on the Left Edge

The airlock stop must be enough for the first row of mashes and the mashes that increase at the left edge.

Increase on the Right Edge

Make enough air stitches at the right edge of the following row before starting.

Slimming on the Edge

If you want to pick up a coin at the beginning of a row, do not pick two, but three, at the last stitch. To take off a coin at the end of a row, grasp the last two loops at once. Or at the beginning, cut off two slings instead of a sling.

Shorten Rows (for Darts)

If different lengths of margins are required, then there are various possibilities, depending on whether the left or the right edge should be shorter. If you want to shorten the left edge, leave the corresponding number of stitches uncoated.

If the right edge should be shorter, then accordingly, on the right edge, leave many loops on the needle. The next is a shortened series after the last short one. Cut off the row at the edge as usual.

Fastening Off

At the end of your piece of crochet, it's important to 'fasten off' your stitches correctly to stop your work unravelling.

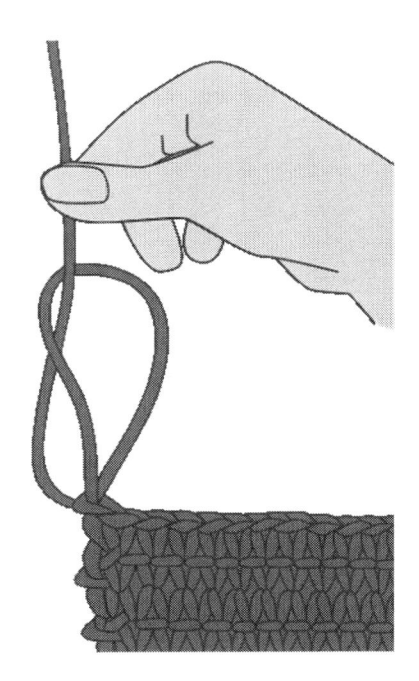

Cut your yarn, leaving a tail of around 10cm/4 in. Loosen the loop of the last stitch, then pull the end of the yarn through that loop all the way, and tighten. You may then want to leave a tail of yarn long enough to sew the item together.

Weaving in Tails Securely

Knowing how to secure the tails of yarn you have from beginning and ending a project, and changing colors is important. You don't want to spend hours of hard work only to have your crochet stitches start to unravel and ruin a project.

I like to weave in the tails from changing colors as I go and not wait until the end of a project. But some folks wait until the end and weave in all of the tails at once, it's up to you how you do it.

Changing Colors

Changing colors in crochet is easy. If you are making stripes, you just add the new color with the first stitch you chain on a new row.

Changing Colors in Single Crochet

I am going to assume you have made a chain and used single crochet to make the first row. In the second row, you single crochet a few stitches until your pattern indicates to change colors in two stitches.

For the last stitch in the old color, insert your hook from front to back into the center V of the next chain or stitch.

Using the new color, wrap it around your hook, and pull it through the two loops on your hook.

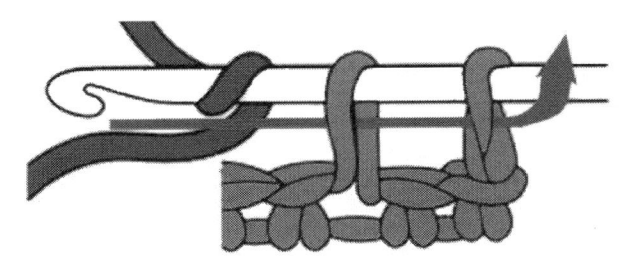

Changing Colors in Double Crochet

The method is the same in the double crochet stitches.

Complete the last stitch you want in the old color right up until you have the last two loops on the hook.

Now, add in the new color, wrap your new color around the hook and pull it through both loops completely the double crochet.

The new color has been started, and the double crochet in the old color has been completed.

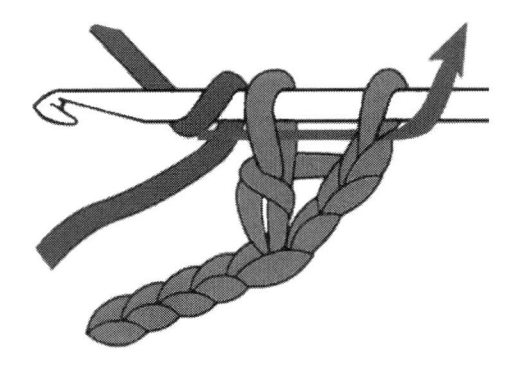

Switching Colors

-Insert the crochet hook into the upcoming stitch and then yarn over:

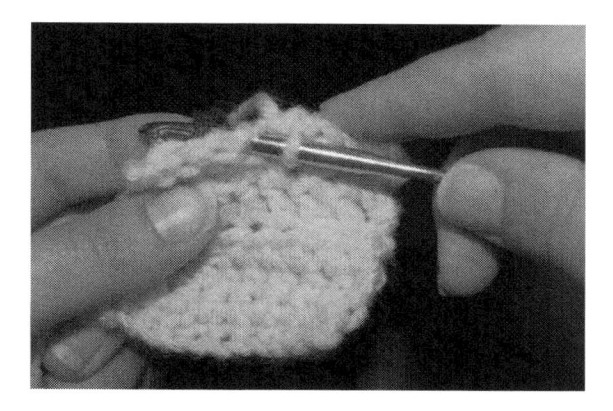

- Gently pull the yarn through only one loop on the crochet hook.

-Now release the loose end of the original color of yarn and hold the new color yarn against the piece of work:

-Yarn over the crochet hook with the new color of yarn that you have selected:

-Gently pull the new color of yarn through the remaining 2 loops left on the crochet hook

-Now, with the new color of yarn, continue your pattern as directed:

Sewing Together

A great way to join crocheted pieces together is by using a technique called the whip stitch.

1. Align the pieces you'd like to join together.

2. Draw the yarn up and over the 2 loops of the first stitch.

3. Repeat the last step through the entire edges to be joined.

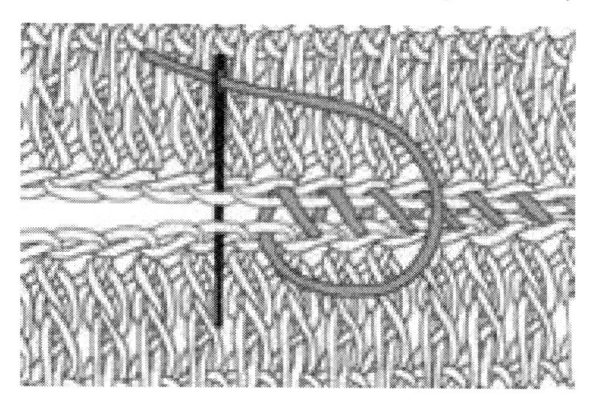

Sewing on Buttons

1. Use a thread that matches your crocheted project.

2. With the back side of your project facing you, slip your needle through a few of the crocheted chains.

3. Pull the thread through until the tail is almost gone and wrap the thread around a single strand of yarn a few times to secure it.

4. Pull your needle through the project to the front in the position that you wish to attach your button.

5. Sew the thread through the button and the project a few times to secure it.

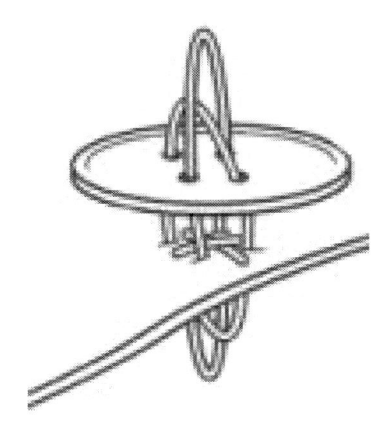

6. Finish at the back of your project, repeating step 3 to secure the button.

Overlay crochet

This is a special color approach that tends to be most widely used in crochet mandala production. It incorporates texture and colour, reminiscent of rich knitwear, mosaics, and stained glass in a special way.

When you can do simple crochet stitches, so you can do crochet overlay. This uses mainly doubles, trebles, and a few unique stitches mean that it might be on the adventurous end of the scale. Although it seems tricky though, it's pretty quick once you get the hang of it!

Overlay crochet also uses different loops at the front and back. You will incorporate your first stitch into the back loop which later leaves the front loop open. Keep your thread, so you can see it on the side, for using the back loop of a stitch. Identify the 'v'-shaped stitches across the top and clearly insert your hook into the back loop just between the' v. DoubleTreble (dtr)

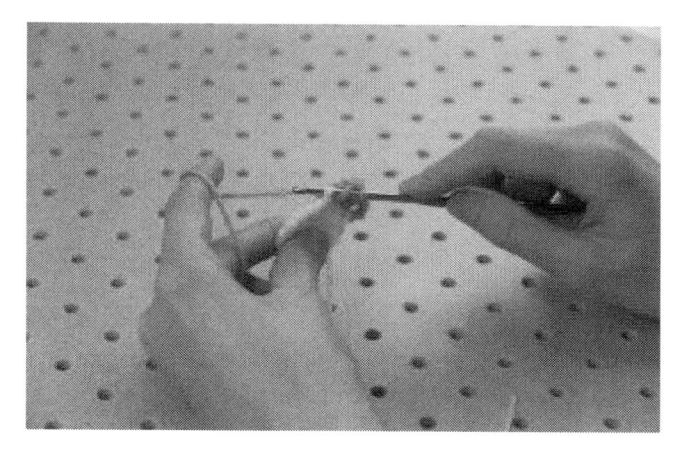

This provides the front loop (FLO) for us to use, having served in the BLO only. This allows for two types of stitches to sit on one side. Because we use the FLO two rows below, we use a good, long stitch like a double treble to ensure that the job is not beveling. Yarn over twice to build the start of the double treble. You'd need to have three hook loops. Double treble process in front loops (FLO).

Insert the hook in the front loops two rows below and yarn over. You're supposed to have 4 loops with your hook. Pull the 2 loops 3 times

This encompasses the development of a sequence of double treble(dtr) and 3 ch. Double treble several times as the pattern is considered for. By altering where you placed the double treble as well as the chain repetitiveness, you can produce different shapes above the top of your MC.

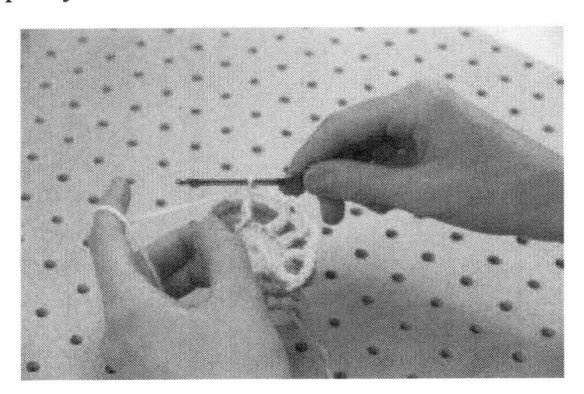

Lace Crochet Techniques

The crochet methodologies in this classification are all varieties of lacy crochet:

Hairpin lace crochet:

Most crochet processes don't necessitate the acquisition of any special equipment; however, the hairpin lace is a bit unusual. You're going to be able to be using the crochet hooks that you already have, but you're also going to go and get your hands on the hairpin lace loom. You may buy an adjustable hairpin lace loom, which actually looks like two linear dowels kept together by two horizontal dowels (sometimes called cross bars) with holes in each of them. To adjust the distance between both the verticals, you can position the vertical dowels in predrilled holes in the horizontal pieces; this is what renders it adjustable.

Create loop with yarn using slipknot and put loop on left rod (counts as the first loop), keep knot in the middle across rods. Yarn end wrap through right rod from front to back, and ball yarn is in front of right rod. Attach hook from bottom to top via loop. Hook yarn and create through loop.

Moving hook to back, making room for wrapping yarn around loom: Drop loop from the hook, with the hook on the back of the frame. Attach hook through the same loop between back to front (just dropped), shift frame clockwise from right to left, hold yarn backed to frame. This helps the yarn to loop across the frame without tangling the hook in the cover, while maintaining the place to stitch the middle further.

Finish 2nd stitch: Insert the hook underneath the line of the left loop, thread over the hook, pull the loop through. Yarn over hook, pull across 2 loops on hook (single crochet created)

Repeat steps 2 and 3 to the required length of strip. rKeep in mind: You crochet 1 knit-per-row vertical crochet in rows.

Filet crochet:

Filet crochet is a simple technique capable of producing spectacular results. Filet crochet patterns are composed of open mesh and solid mesh variations depicting this (therefore the patterns are crochet graphs, not written guidelines).

The mesh is crafted from double crochet (solid blocks) stitches isolated by spaces (active blocks). The blocks can also be created using either 3dc or 4 dc stitches, depends entirely on the filet crochet version that you are working with. This guide discusses both but explicitly demonstrates how to work with 4 dc crochet filets, as this is the most common of the two approaches. (Vercillo, Learn the Basics of Filet Crochet, 2019)

Filet Crochet Patterns Are Blocks

The very first thing you need to remember about crochet filets is that you won't have any documented directions for those designs. You physically can't have maps with words, either. Alternatively, you will also have grids; the grids will comprise of spaces "open" and spaces "tight." To establish the open boxes you utilize double crochet stitches to build the strong spaces and attach chains over skipped stitches.

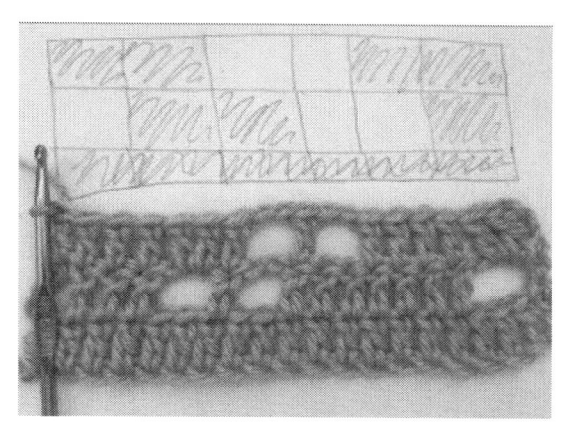

3 DC vs 4 DC Blocks for Filet Crochet

Many designs use 4 dc to shape a block (solid mesh), while others use 3 dc (solid mesh) to shape a block.

3 DC filet explained: Each block comprises of 3 dc in a design which uses 3 double crochet (dc) to shape each block (solid mesh). The blocks share some common dc in the center if there are two blocks next to each other so there will be 5 dc within this unit of two blocks. Three blocks next to each will be equal to 7 dc.

4 DC filet explained: Every block consisting of 4 dc in a design which uses 4 double crochet (dc) to create each block (solid mesh). The blocks share a similar dc in the middle because there are two blocks next to each other and there will be 7 dc in the that unit of two blocks. Three blocks beside each other are equal to 10 dc.

If you're puzzled, take the time to examine the filet crochet graph maps. Each row is composed of blocks. Any block is free, or firm. Double crochet stitches are used to fill a solid block in. When mentioned above, you use three dc stitches, or 4 dc stitches. Through block shares a solid white line with both the block beside it so that the first block's last stitch will be the next block's first stitch. That's why two 4dc blocks beside each other won't have 8 dc and will have 7 dc instead, since block 1 consists of 1-4 dc stitches and block 2 consists of 4-7 dc stitches. They both have four stitches on the dc but share the center.

Making Solid Crochet Squares in Filet Crochet

The X, or totally filled in block, on a map is equivalent to a solid mesh. The symbol reveals what the strong mesh looks like on a diagram of stitch symbols. To create a solid mesh: dc for next 3 dc or 2 dc for next chain area, dc for next dc. The starting solid mesh is composed of: ch 3 (classifies as dc), 2 dc during the first row, dc over the next dc or dc during the next 3 dc. Notice that several (though not all) crochet filet techniques may start and end with a whole row of double crochet stitches, as this gives the design a pleasant frame.

Making Open Mesh Squares in Filet Crochet

The empty square on a map represents an open mesh. The symbol indicates how the open mesh looks like on a diagram of stitch symbols. To create an open mesh: ch2, skip 2 chains next, dc in the next dc or skip 2 dc next, dc in next dc. The Starting Open Mesh is rendered by: ch 5, skip next 2 stitches, dc in next dc.

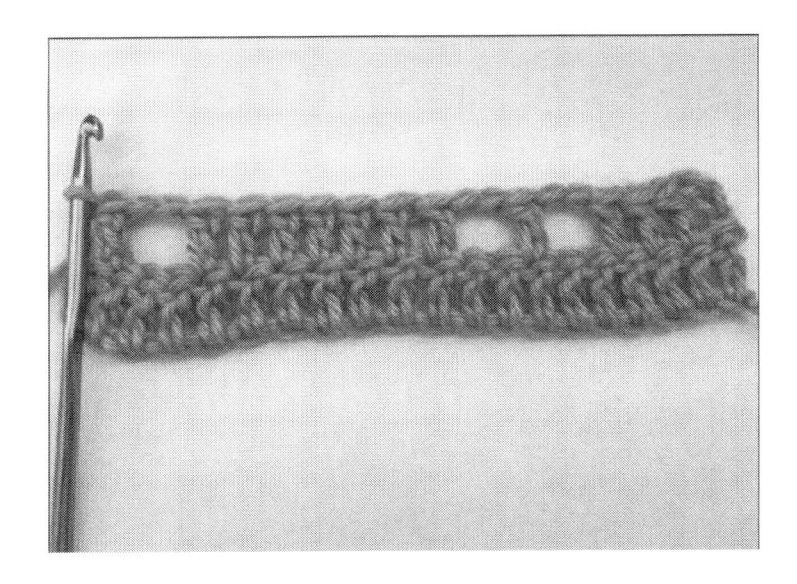

Calculating Your Starting Chains for Filet Crochet

We spoke about how to make open and solid mesh stitching in the beginning but how do you start the whole project. Of course you must have a starting line.

Initially, calculate the number of boxes you will be focused on the diagram for the first row. Diagrams are typically starting at the bottom of the graph. Most edgings are operated sideways (the short rows), and you can determine the length as you move along.

First, decide whether you want a 3 dc meshes or a 4 dc meshes map to operate on. 3 dc mesh is equal to a mesh consisting 3 dc for each mesh (that last dc of a mesh always counts as the very first dc of another mesh after that first mesh). 4 dc mesh is equal to a mesh consisting 4 dc for each mesh (the last dc of a mesh are always counted as the first dc of another mesh after that first mesh).

How to Filet Crochet

The crochet design bookmark tells the following on how to interpret a crochet pattern for filets:

Each solid square is exactly equivalent to a "block" of "dc for next dc, dc for next 2 sts or ch-2, dc for next dc." Each open square is equivalent to a "space" of "dc, ch 2, skip next 2 sts, dc." The dc at the end of each square is often known to be the first dc of another block or space. One block accompanied by a space is equal to dc in next 4 sts, ch 2, skip next 2 sts, dc in next dc.

That's about true. If you have never performed any crochet filet work, though, it can be somewhat frustrating. But let's overlook it.

That's what you have to learn about filets crochet:

Only double crochet stitches and chain stitches are used to carry out the whole fabric.

The pattern is diagram. The diagram is a series of blocks. Both double crochet stitches will be blocks which are filled in. Open blocks would be two stitches of a chain with a dc on each side.

The crochet map for filets is read from either the bottom up. Row 1, at the bottom of the picture.

Odd-numbered rows are handled from right to left but even number rows are handled from left to right. That is important for people to know whenever working on asymmetric designs.

The cloth you make is sometimes referred to as "mesh" or "grid ». Techniques often apply to open mesh blocks and closed mesh ones. One may also name open blocks empty or hollow. Filled-in blocks can also be labeled solid blocks, or squares generally.

Usually, each row begins and ends with a "closed mesh" or solid block square (four double crochets) instead of open spaces, although that might vary according to design.

Now here's the most important thing that can often get missed by people new to filet crochet. Since there are four stitches in each crochet block, most of those stitches are distributed among blocks.

A crochet block is filled in with 4 double crochet stitches. When you have two filled-in blocks in a design next to one another then in fact there are seven double crochet stitches, not 8. That's because the first block's last double crochet is the second block's 1st double crochet. Likewise, when you have a block filled (four double crochet stitches) beside an open block (dc, chain 2 and sk 2, double chain) you'll find four double crochet stitches, a chain 2 room, and one double crochet. This is because the last dc of the first block seems to be the second (open) block's first double crochet.

Here's what an entirely open mesh block should look like

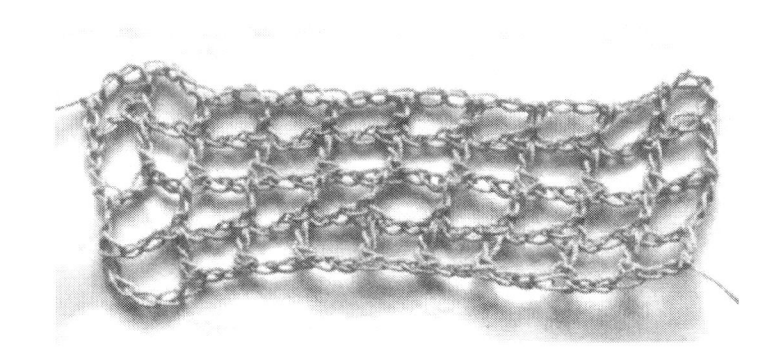

Now note that we normally begin and end with solid blocks so we will "fill in" certain rows by incorporating two double crochets in the first and last spaces of the chain:

We will then look at how it looks as if we incorporate other boxes to "fill in" in double crochets:

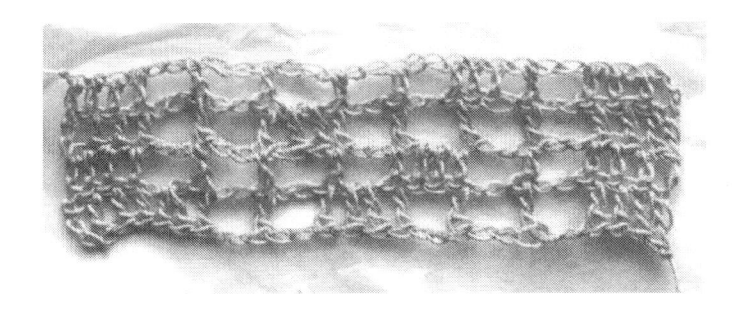

Broomstick Lace Crochet

Broomstick lace is a crochet pattern that has its own. The pattern is created using a crochet hook to pull large thread loops upward to a dowel (historically a broomstick, through which the term comes). Those loops are made around the row from left to right. They are often looped into clusters utilizing single crochet stitches that operated from back to left around the loops. There are lots of variants of lace crochet broomstick however once you learn the fundamentals you can easily master the variants. Below we'll see how to crochet simple broomstick lace piece by piece and then maybe we can cover a few of the variants and supplementary tips to help you with the design. (Sams, n.d.)

How to Crochet Broomstick Lace

Crochet a chain at the top. The initial chain must be as much loops as you wish for all of the lace rows of your broomstick, plus another one to be used as a turning chain. In this example, we need five clusters with four loops each (20 total loops) so we're going to build a 20 + 1 starting chain (total 21).

Broomstick lace is designed from left to right and you have to crochet all over the base row and get back to the left side and start the design. Single crochet from either the hook in to the second chain, though for a total of 20 sc every chain across. (Sams, n.d.)

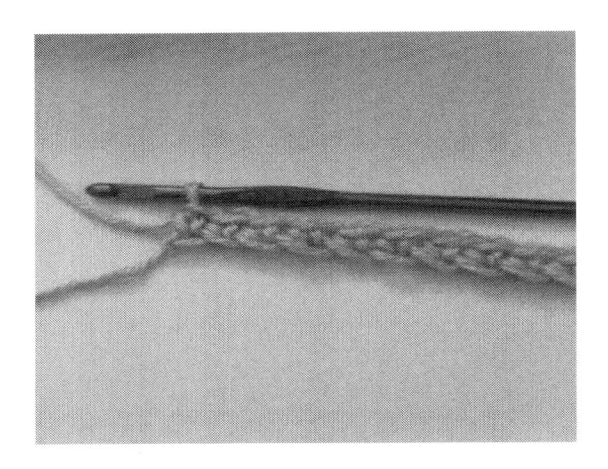

Embed your crochet needle on only the left side of that same row into first sc. Yarn over, and make a loop. End up making the loop as high as the lace stitches on the broomstick should be. For that kind of example, the loops are drawn right up to the edge of the Q hook which is used to hold the loops. Slip the loop (or dowel) across the Q loop to secure it in there.

4. Pull the crochet hook from work, hang onto the Q hook or dowel the current loop. Push the hook crochet through left across second sc.

Create a further loop then slip it over your Q hook

Repeat the cycle of forming loops, and keep these all the way around the row on the Q hook.

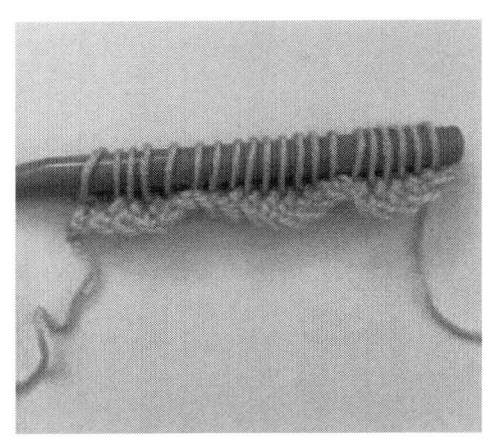

Take the hook off the job. To retain their height, safely slide the first four loops (on the right hand side of the job) off the Q handle. Connect all four loops with the hook.

Yarn over and pull via the four loops. Make one chain for a pivoting chain.

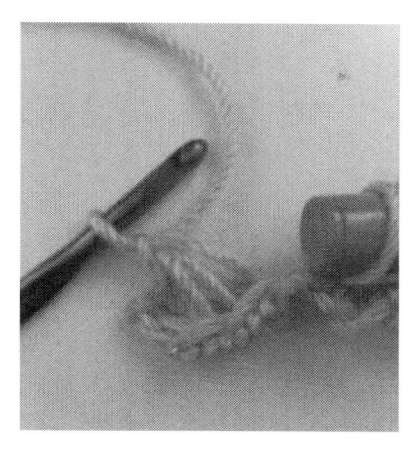

Sc four stitch at the very same location (equals the number of loops that you are dealing with).

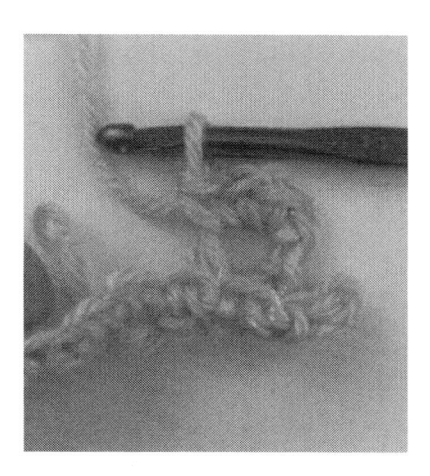

Working back through the row via right to left, go on sliding four loops out of the Q hook at one time, onto the hook and lock them with four sc each. (There is no need for a rotating chain on all of these, maybe the first cluster).

Look at your job right now and you'll see you've got 20 sc stitches lying on top of that first row of broomstick lace. Now you'll repeat steps 3-7 to build many more rows of broomstick lace as you need to. (Sams, n.d.)

Bruges Lace Crochet

Bruges lace is a method originating in Belgium using structure consisting of a ribbon / tape and chains on each section of the tape producing the lacy effect. This lace production method is actually very basic, but it can yield fantastic results both alone and when combined with other crochet practices.

Making the tape

On its most simple, Bruges lace is a single-stitch "tape" or column, with chain loops hanging out at the beginning of each row. Here you can see a straight tape forming the loop, in which each row is ch 5, and afterwards 3 dc.

The loops will switch on each side of the tape, as you switch your stuff back and forth for each row. You can develop lace that twists and bends to make different designs by changing the stitch used, and linking the loops together. (Scraps, 2017)

Making curves

Using tiny stitches at one end and bigger stitches on the other, to create the tape curves. The tape bends into the tiny stitches. Here you can see that the rows are single crochet at the inside edge of the arc, half double crochet at the middle thread, and dc at the outside. At first, every row still has a loop. These loops at the inside of the curve are linked together at the center.

Joining loops

The tape is operated straight up again after the curve, on the other side. The loops on the inside are also linked together, making the look of lattice. Do not ch 5, then ch 2, slip stitch in the loop to which you wish to join, and ch 2 once more to create a joining loop. The slip stitch counts as the loop's 3rd ch and you get a (ch 2, slip stitch, chain 2) loop rather than a ch 5 loop.

Making Pom Poms

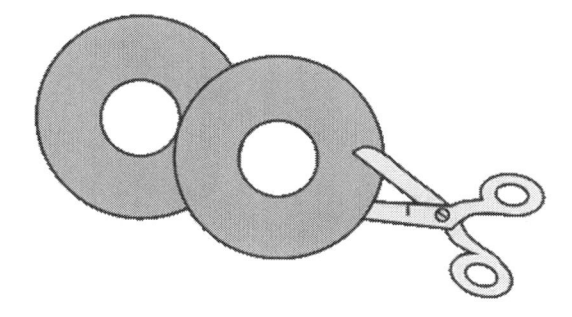

Step 1: How large would you like your pom pom? Find a jar lid, CD or something of similar size and draw around it on the cardboard. Now draw a smaller circle inside the large one. Repeat this, so that you cut two cardboard "donuts" that are both the same.

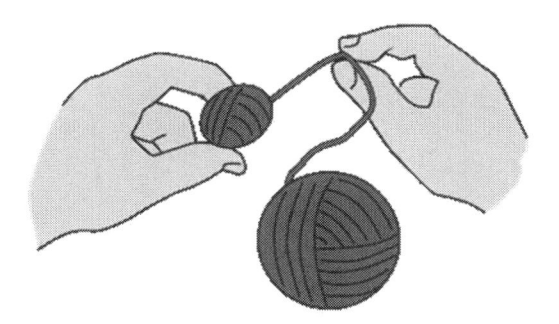

Step 2: If you are using a large ball of yarn, it will be too big to pass through the hole, so make a small ball that will fit by winding the yarn around your fingers lots of times. Stop before it is too large to fit through the hole.

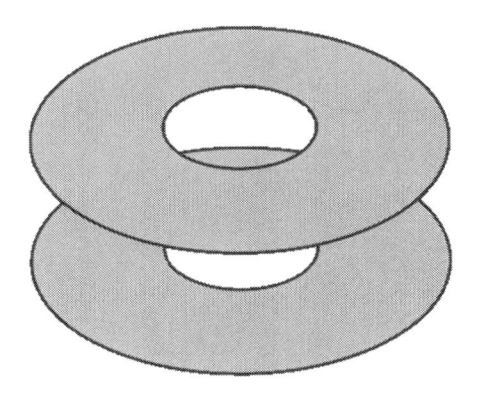

Step 3: Now put both discs together. You're now ready to start winding your yarn around the discs.

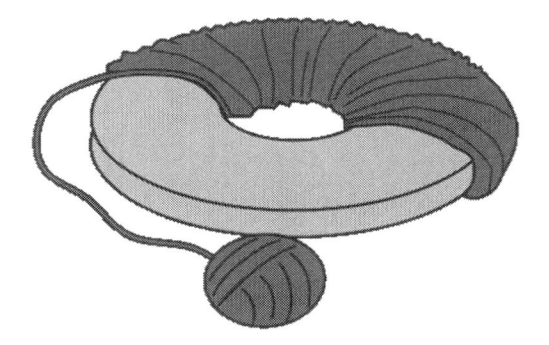

Step 4: Holding the two discs together, start winding your yarn over the disc and through the hole, repeating again and again until you have covered the whole disc in yarn. Keep repeating this until the hole is too small for any more yarn to pass through.

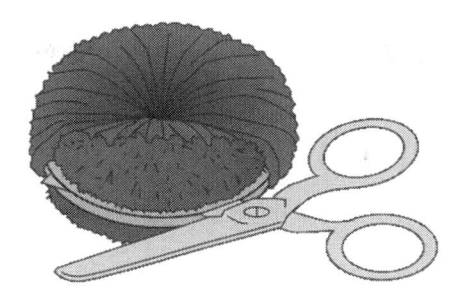

Step 5: Carefully insert one blade of your scissors between the two discs, and start cutting through the yarn. Keep moving the scissors around the edge, cutting the yarn as you go, until you have cut all the way around.

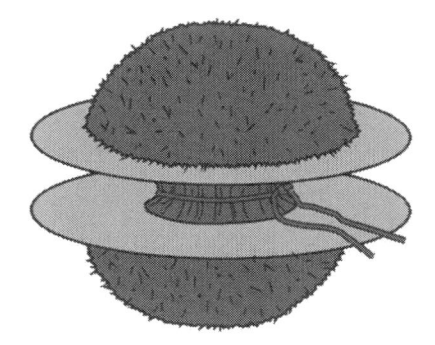

Step 6: Cut a length of yarn and carefully pull apart the two discs slightly. Wrap your yarn between the two discs and around the middle of your pom pom, and tie in a tight knot. Do this a couple more times so that your pom pom is really secure. Now rip or cut each disc away, and roll your pom pom between your hands to hide the join and make it nice and fluffy!

Crochet with Plastic Rings

Pure fun brings crocheting with plastic rings. A brisk job that brings results quickly. However, you should not crochet the rings individually but create coherent chains.

Making a Crochet Ring

To start, put the normal crochet start loop on the plastic ring. The loop for the first solid ash and all subsequent hands is always pulled through the ring. Then, as usual, the two loops that are on the needle are embraced with an envelope. Repeat this until the ring is completely crocheted. Before you start work, crochet a ring completely to the sample to know how many units are needed overall. This is also dependent on wool strength.

Connect Rings Together

The connection between two rings takes place when the first plastic ring is crocheted in half with solid hands. Now, crochet an air mesh and then the first solid mesh around the next ring.

The last ring of a row is always completely crocheted. All other half-finished crocheted rings will be completed in the second round with solid hands. In doing so, always crochet a solid piece of ash around the connecting air mesh. In the end, pull the thread through the last stitch and sew it.

The second row of rings can now also be half crocheted and connected to the rings of the first row. When crocheting the first half of the second row of rings, add the already finished first row of rings. To do this, crochet a slit stitch into the middle stitch of the already finished ring row.

The crochet with plastic rings is particularly suitable for original placemats, small coasters, and the design of fabric bags, which receive such a special design. Of course, all these suggestions are also suitable for individual gifts.

Crochet Flowers

These flowers are crocheted with wool for a crochet hook of strength 4 in rounds, and each of them is closed with a Kettmasche.

- Close the chain of 6 meshes with a chain stitch to the ring.

- 1*st* round: 12 fixed sts.

- 2*nd* round: in every M. 2 tr. (Replace the first trump with 3 ch.).

- 3*rd* round: Instead of the first tr. 3 ch., Then into the first st. 1 tr., In the next M. Crochet 1 tr and 1 half tr

At the following 4 m. in each puncture site 1 solid st., 1 half st. and 1 st., then 2 st., in the 4. Crochet 1 tr and 1 half tr.

Repeat 4 times and replace the 6*th* sheet with 1 solid M., 1 complete half tr. and 1 tr. Cut the thread and pull it through. You can combine several individual motifs into one flower, or you can stitch together two individual motifs in different colors. Thus, simple blankets and crocheted with raffia, even carpets.

Buttonholes

The incorporation of buttonholes is parallel to the series course performed. For each skipped ash, an envelope is picked up.

In the second step, two loops or slings and an envelope. The drawing at the bottom right shows how to make the loops in the next row above the buttonhole. If you do not want the buttonhole to be crocheted horizontally, you have to divide the work in the size of the buttonhole (3–4 m.). Crochet at the edge over the desired number of rows. Then crochet the other side with a new thread.

Horizontal Buttonhole

For this example, we are using single crochet. However, you would use this same technique with other stitches.

First Row: Work your stitches into where the buttonhole will be. You will then skin the number of stitches needed for the diameter of the buttonhole. Chain the number of stitches that you skipped. For this example, we skipped 5, so we chained 5. After you chain, continue the row of the first stitch after the stitches you skipped.

Second Row: You will crochet the regular pattern across the row over the chain stitches. You will then continue working your pattern as directed.

Loop Buttonhole

We are using a single crochet; however, you would use this same technique with other stitches.

1. You will begin this on the last row or while you are edging.
2. Find where you would like to have your buttonhole. Skip the number of stitches so that it equals the correct diameter for the button. You will then chain the same number of stitches that you skipped. For this example, we skipped 5, so we chained 5.
3. Turn the work over to make sure that the chain is doubled back. Then slip stitch into the last stitch; in this case, the last stitch is a single crochet.
4. Now, single crochet over each of the chains.

Tip: The piece's integrity needs to have the exact number of single crochets as you have chains.

To finish off the loop, simply slip stitch over the next stitch and continue to the pattern as directed.

Making Ridges

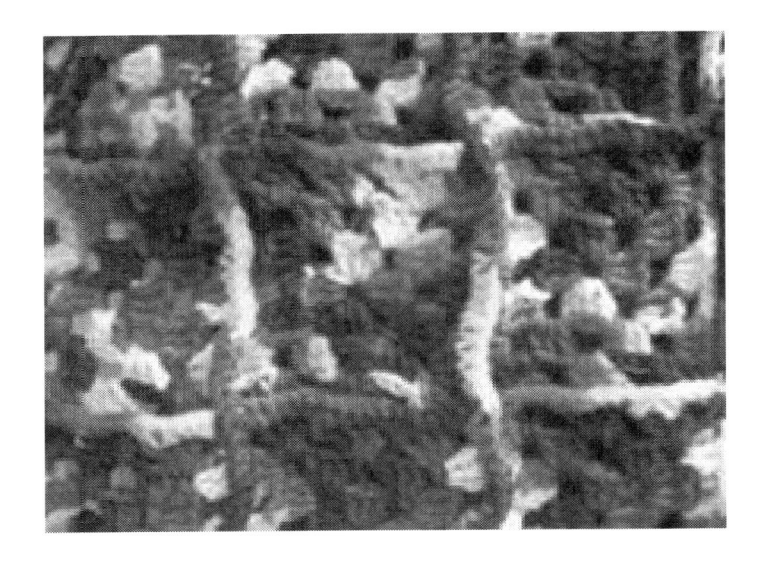

Ridges can be crocheted for a number of reasons; to add detail to a design, to finish something off nicely, or even to give a textured effect. To do this, you need to:

1. Make your slip knot stitch and create your foundation chain.

2. Start with a double crochet stitch and repeat this along the row.
3. Create a slip stitch in the turning chain to end this row.

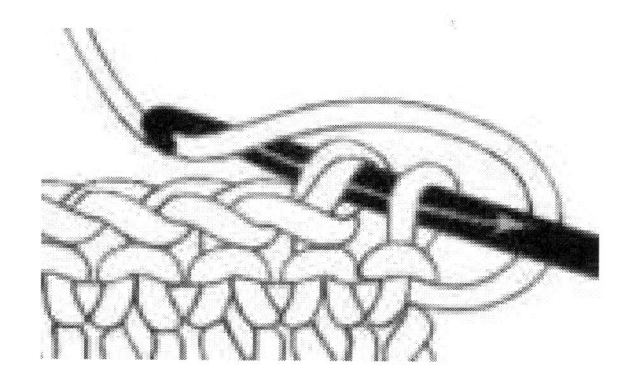

4. Chain 3 stitches and skip the first stitch to create a double crochet stitch in the back loop of the second stitch away from the hook.

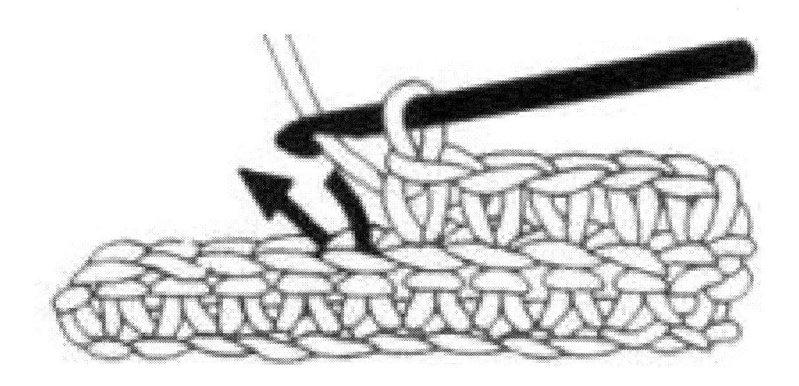

Shell Borders

Shell borders are very popular as they give a crochet project a pretty edge, without being too fussy or difficult to do. To crochet a shell stitch:

1. Make a slip knot and crochet your foundation chain.
2. Work in a single crochet stitch into the second chain from your hook.

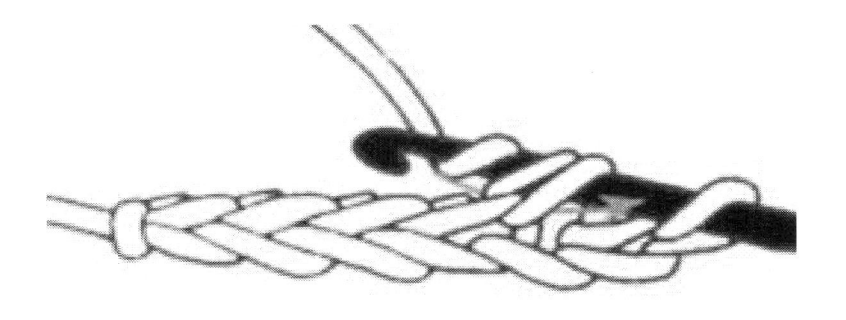

Working a Square

1. Make a slip knot and create your foundation chain.

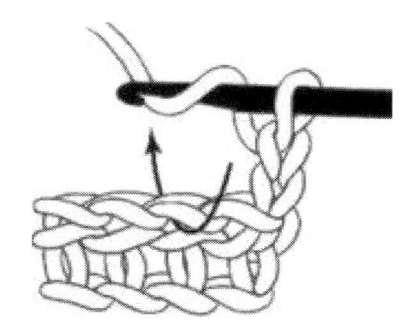

2. Create a half-double crochet stitch.

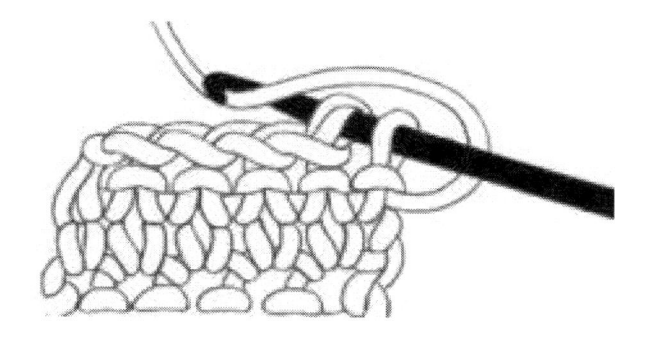

3. Turn your work at the end of the row and repeat steps 2 and 3.
4. Repeat step 4 until the square is complete.

Edgings

Creating edgings to finish off your projects adds a neat finish. There are numerous edgings you can make which involve the use of basic stitches.

Simple Edging

Let's try a simple one:

You'll need to crochet five rows for this edging.

Begin with a foundation chain, which should be in four multiples, for example, 20 stitches.

Row 1: Do a single chain into the second chain from your hook, then one single crochet in each chain thereafter.

Rows 2–4: Work one chain stitch, then one single crochet in every Ch stitch until the row's end.

Row 5: Work three chain stitches, then skip one single crochet then work one double chain into the following single chain, work 3 chain stitches, then work 3 double chain stitches over the double chain you've just made. * Skip three single crochet stitches, work one double chain into the next double chain, crochet 3 chain stitches, then 3 double chain stitches over the double chain you just made, repeat from * until the end but finish the row with the following: one single chain, then one double crochet into the last single crochet. After all that you can fasten off your work.

Even Edges

One of the biggest complaints I hear from beginners is that their edges aren't even. One side grows while the other one shrinks. The easiest way to prevent this is to count the stitches in each row as you work them. This way you have the correct number of stitches and your rows will be even.

Another way to ensure your edges are even is to end each row into the top of the turning chain of the previous row. For example, if you're working with single crochet, then the last stitch is worked in chain 1 of the turning chain of the previous row.

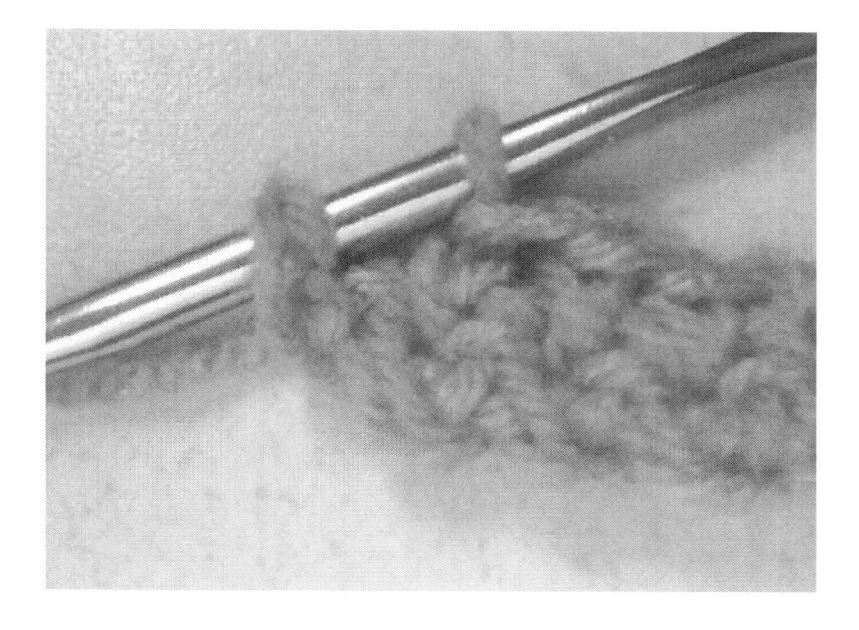

Always catch both loops of the chain stitch in the last stitch to secure the stitch and stabilize it. If you're working with double crochet, then the last stitch of the row is worked into the third chain of the turning chain, and so on. When you begin a row always crochet the first stitch into the next stitch after the turning chain, not in the base of the turning chain.

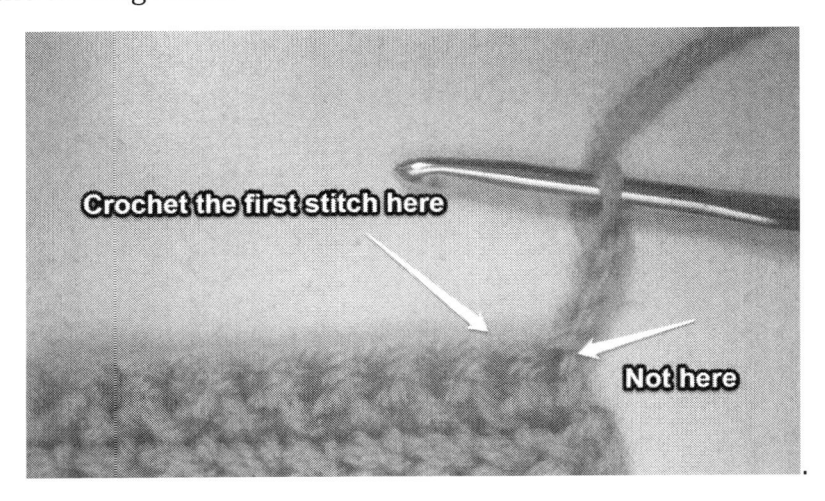

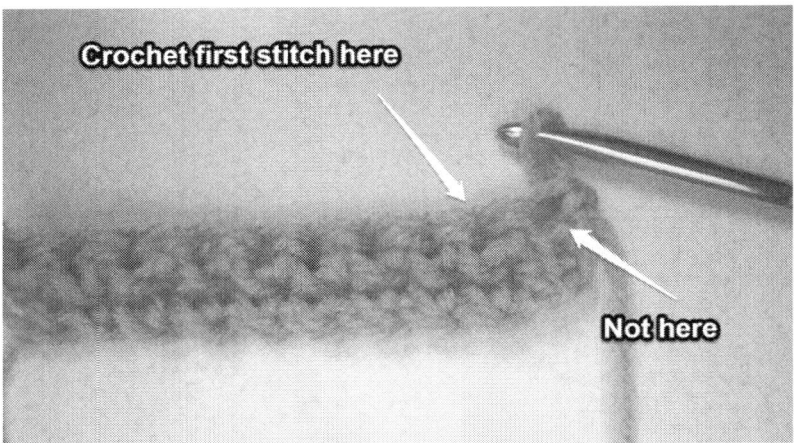

Crab Stitch Edgings

You can't go wrong with this edging; it is easy to make and also rather versatile and hardy. Try it and see how it goes, it is practically the same as doing a single crochet, the only difference being that you'll be working from left to right as you crochet.

262

Simple instructions to follow:

1. Join the yarn you have to the first stitch then draw a loop.
2. Using your crochet hook, turn it around so it inserts into the stitch on the right instead of the left.
3. Your hook should be on the other side now and you'll need to adjust it so that you draw your working yarn through. The hook should point in a downwards direction to make it easier to hook the yarn.
4. And that is one crab stitch completed.
5. Your hook needs to be turned backward now so you can stick it into your stitch that is to your right. And now you can repeat steps 3 to 5 once again. Carry on and finish your round.
6. Once you come to the start, you should turn your crochet hook, then put it into the exact place where you made that first chain stitch of yours.
7. Now, complete the crab stitch, then finish fastening off.
8. Crochet in your loose end on the wrong side of your work for a few cm before cutting the yarn.

How to Create a Clean Edge for a Decorative Border

When you complete a project like an afghan and you want to add a decorative border crochet a round of single crochet around the edge to create a nice even border to work with.

When you work along the edges you will have to estimate the number of stitches you will need and place them according to the type of stitches that were used in your project. For example, I find two single crochet stitches along the side of a double crochet works very well.

Three stitches are worked in the corners so that you get a nice sharp corner. When you go around the corner again work the next three stitches into the middle stitch of the corner. This keeps your corners sharp and in the correct place.

Working in Rows

In short, this simply means working back and forth from one side to the other.

You will want to rely on your pattern here because it will tell you how many to chain. For this example, we will use a single crochet.

Let's say your pattern asked you to chain 10:

1. You will then single crochet in the first chain from the hook and all the following chains:

2. Now turn your work and chain 1:

3. Now single crochet in all stitches, starting with the 2nd stitch from the hook; unless directed otherwise by the pattern:

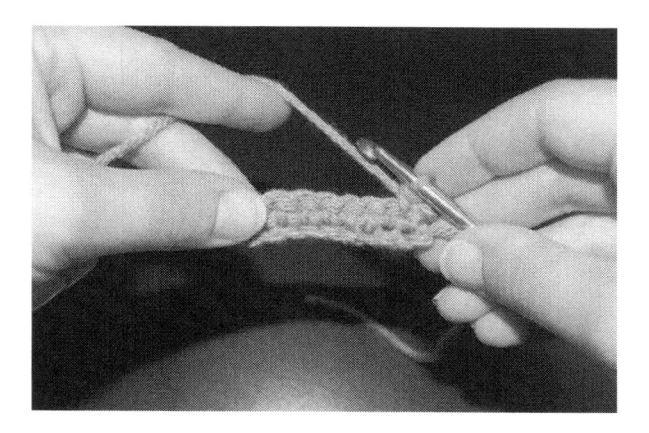

Blocking Your Crochet

Blocking is a vital part of the crochet process as it is the part that makes your projects look professional. It is sometimes termed as "dressing" the project and we use moisture and sometimes heat to finish it. If you are making garments, correct blocking can go an awful and long way towards making the garment fit properly and making it look better. It can also help Afghans or rugs that have warped regain their symmetry.

Blocking sets the stitches in place and enhance the way the fabric drapes. It is much easier to seam and edge on a blocked piece and, if needed, you can also make any minor adjustments to size while you are blocking as well.

There are a few different methods to blocking crochet and you need to know which one works for the project you need to block, otherwise, your result will not be what you expect and you could find that all your hard work has gone to waste.

The method you use depends on the item itself and the yarn or thread that has been used to crochet it. Some items cannot be blocked, like 3D pieces that are not easy to handle, or very small items. Some fibers are not ideal for blocking either.

Getting Started

You will need:

- A blocking board—must be flat and large enough to hold what you want to block. Pieces should not be allowed to hang off the edge of the blocking board

- Rustproof pins—important—if you don't get the rustproof ones, you might find rust marks on your work when you have finished blocking
- Steamer or steam iron
- Spray bottle
- The labels from your yarn or thread

If you can't find or your budget doesn't allow a commercial blocking board, you can easily make one. When you are choosing which size to buy, keep in mind that while a huge board can be used to block several pieces, it is more difficult to store. Perhaps consider buying several boards of different sizes.

Cover the board over with a thick towel and then a cotton cloth or cotton sheet. Do wash both of these first to ensure that they do not "bleed" onto your work. Solid white is often the best color to go for but you can use a fabric that has stripes or a large check print so that you can use the lines as a guide for your blocking.

Place your board in a room where it can be left undisturbed while you are blocking. This might be just a few minutes or it can be an entire day or 2, depending on the size of the piece and the yarn used. The board must be able to take pins, heat, and moisture. If you have large items, like large Afghans or blankets, you could use a bed or a padded dining room table. If not, you can always cover part of a carpeted floor in a sheet and use that.

Blocking Methods

You may hear of blocking methods being described as wet, cold, or dry. The method you choose will depend on the content of the yarn, the final use, and your preferred method.

The first step is to look at the label that came with the yarn to see what fibers have been used. Sometimes a skein will contain many different fibers and, if that is the case, the most delicate of the fibers must take precedence. Most of the natural fibers, like wool, cotton, mohair, or linen, can be wet or dry blocked. Some of the synthetic fibers do not gain any benefit from being blocked and can be ruined if you are not careful. If you have used metallic or novelty fibers, these need special attention and might not be able to be blocked at all.

If possible, make up a test swatch of the yarn you are using to check the gauge and to practice blocking on. This will ensure that you are using the right method for it. If you are using acrylic yarn, it might interest you to know that too much heat can actually "kill it," making it go limp and shiny. It's better to ruin your swatch than your project!

Wet Blocking

Wet blocking can only be used on fibers that can be submerged in water. Wash your swatch and see what happens to it. If the material does not hold up to washing, it cannot be wet blocked. If you are ready to start wet blocking, wash the piece first or wet it thoroughly and squeeze the excess water out gently. Do not twist or wring the material.

If the piece is 2D, lay it out flat on the blocking board, and pat it into shape gently. Make sure you shape it to the dimensions you want it to be when finished because once the blocking is over, it can't be undone.

Dry Blocking

Dry blocking can be used on those fibers that can take both moisture and heat in the form of steam. Pin the piece onto the board in your desired shape or measurements. Keep the pins close together and spaced out evenly so the fabric does not get distorted.

Cold Blocking

Cold blocking is ideal for those fibers that can tolerate moisture but can't tolerate heat. Pin the piece to the board in the same way as you did for dry blocking. Fill a spray bottle with clean water and mist it over the piece until it is completely wet. Use extra pins if there are areas that refuse to lie flat or press them down with your (clean) hands for a minute. Leave it until it is dry.

Blocking Tips for Large Pieces

Large pieces, such as Afghans, blankets, tablecloths, or shawls, can be blocked on a bed that has a good firm or extra-firm mattress. You can also pad your dining table with a blanket and cover it or use a covered clean floor with carpet.

Arrange your piece so it is a nice and even shape. Do not overstretch it and do not distort the shape. Pin it down securely, keeping the pins evenly spaced but close together. Add some extra pins to stubborn bits that just won't lie flat.

Dry block or block with no heat. Use the instructions above for dry blocking or you can mist it thoroughly with chemical-free water until it is semi-saturated (not sopping wet). Use your hand to press each area as you spray it and let the heat from your skin act as iron at low temperatures. This is a great way of blocking without the damage that can be caused by iron.

Once you have wet and hand-pressed it, set up a fan to blow over it gently until it is dry.

Working in the Round

If you want to crochet a hat or a purse or even a drink coaster, you will need to know how to crochet in the round.

We will use the single crochet as our example to get started. Many patterns begin working in the round with single crochet.

Beginning Your Round

To begin crochet in the round, you must begin with a center ring. This ring is the foundation, and all of your stitches radiate out from it. There are some different methods to do this. We will begin with working your chain stitches into a ring.

Make a slip knot on your hook.

Chain six stitches.

Slip stitch the chain together.

You have now joined the chain into a ring.

The number of stitches in your chain determines the size of the hole that the center ring creates, and also how many stitches you can work into that center ring. The pattern you are working on should indicate how many stitches to make in your chain, but you can adjust it larger to smaller if you find the hole is too big or too small.

You are ready to crochet your first circular round, but first, you need to determine the number of turning chains you will need.

Remember: we must always bring our yarn up to the correct level for the next row of stitches. In this case, we are using single crochet, so we know that we will require one turning chain.

Chain one. This is your turning chain for single crochet.

Insert your hook through the center of the ring.

Yarn over your hook.

Pull the yarn through the center ring so you now have two loops on your hook.

Yarn over the hook.

Pull the yarn through the two loops on your hook.

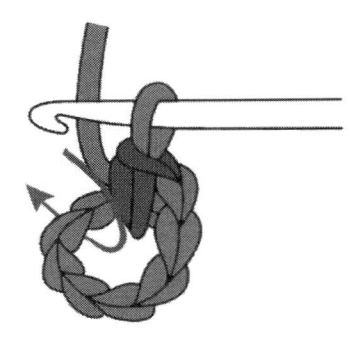

You have completed your first single crochet into the ring. Continue to work single crochet stitches into the ring until you have completed ten, including your chain one.

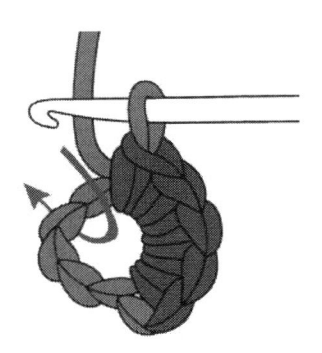

To join your round of single crochet stitches into a ring ready for the second round of stitches, this is what to do:

Skip the chain one turning the chain you made and insert your hook under the top two loops of the first single crochet stitch you made.

Yarn over the hook.

You are now ready to begin adding rounds to your first row of circular crochet. It is similar to adding rows except you do not turn your work, you go around and around. Also, you need to increase the number of stitches you work on in every round.

Otherwise, your crochet work will not lie flat but become a sort of thimble shape. The pattern you are working with will tell you how often to increase. You will make more increases using double and treble crochet because those stitches are long and they increase the circumference of a circle more quickly than single crochet.

4 Steps to Work the Second Round of Single Crochet

After joining your first round, chain one stitch for the turning chain.

Do not turn your work. Work two single crochet stitches under the top two loops of the first stitch. (This is the same stitch you worked your slip stitch into.)

Work two single crochet stitches in each stitch all the way around the circle. You are increasing all the way around; your stitch count will double.

Slip stitch the first and last stitch of the round together.

Now make a practice circle of single crochet for your sample collection. Remember you will need to increase stitches every round to keep your work flat. You can experiment with increasing every stitch, or you could increase on every other stitch or every third stitch.

If you have trouble seeing the first stitch at the beginning of a row, simply put a safety pin or a crochet marker through that stitch, so you will know when you have come around to it and complete your circle with a slip stitch.

Working in Round with Double or Treble Crochet

When working in the round with double crochet or any stitch other than single crochet:

Chain the beginning of the round. (In our example you chain ten stitches.)

Join those stitches into a circle by using a slip stitch, as illustrated above in the single crochet instructions.

Single crochet around the circle, creating as many stitches as your pattern calls for.

Now chain 3 to bring the yarn up to the correct level to begin your double crochet round.

For round two you are going to double crochet twice into each single crochet stitch of the previous round. This will double the number of stitches in your round, and it will lie flat.

Once you have completed your first row of double crochet stitches, slip stitch into the top of the turning chain to complete the round.

Invisible Join Method

Usually, when you crochet in the round, the joining seam is quite noticeable. It runs up the fabric diagonally because of the way the stitch counts end up and it is perfectly normal. Instead of having a noticeable seam, use the invisible join method to create a practically invisible seam. Work the correct number of stitches in the round. Work one more stitch in the same space as the starting chain. Instead of joining in the appropriate chain stitch, join in the next stitch. This hides the starting chain and since you worked one extra stitch, your stitch counts come out correctly.

Working in a Spiral

If you crochet in a circle but do not end the round with a slip stitch, what happens is that you create a rounded spiral shape. Spirals are often used for simple things like coasters, or the bottom of a crocheted basket. Here is how to create a continuously growing spiral.

Chain the beginning of the round. (In our example you chain 8 stitches.) Join those stitches into a circle by using a slip stitch, as illustrated above in the single crochet instructions.

Round 1: Chain 1, nine single crochet into the ring.

Round 2: Make two single crochet into every stitch on this round. Total of 18 stitches.

Round 3: Make two single crochet into the next stitch, single crochet into the next stitch. Repeat this nine times. Total of 27 stitches.

Round 4: Make two single crochet into the next stitch, single crochet into the following two stitches. Repeat this nine times. Total of 36 stitches.

Round 5: Make two single crochet in the next stitch, single crochet in the next three stitches. Repeat this nine times. Total of 45 stitches.

Round 6: Make two single crochet in the next stitch, single crochet in the next four stitches. Repeat this nine times. Total of 54 stitches. You will notice that in the spiral we have created nine increases (single crochet twice into the same stitch) in each round. And each round has one more single crochet between increases than the previous round. You can keep going with this established pattern to make a spiral as large as you wish.

Backstitch Seam Joining

1. Start by holding the two pieces of work right sides together. To keep them steady, you may want to tack them together while you work. You will need a darning needle to backstitch, and you will work from right to left.

2. Insert the darning needle straight through the work from the top piece of work to the bottom.
3. Then reinsert the darning needle from the bottom to top in stitch 2 ahead:

4. Then insert the darning needle where your last stitch ended; each stitch will be worked halfway through the previous stitch. You will continue the previous technique until you reach the end of the row:

Tip: This may result in a bulky thick seam.

How to Work a Front Post

For this lesson, we will use dc to create fpdc. When you want to raise a crochet stitch, you need to use front post stitches. Start where your double crochet lesson ended.

1. You have one row of finished dc stitches. Turn your work (see figure 1 under Turning Chain) and continue with the next row (see figure 2 under Turning Chain). Use ch-2 as your turning chain instead of 3. Fpdc stitches are shorter than the normal dc stitches.
2. Yarn over and slip your hook from the front going to the back of the next post (the post beneath the row that you are currently working on) and to the front again.

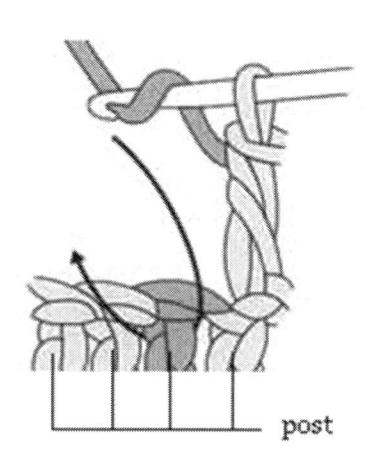

post

3. Hook a thread and lead it back to your starting position. You should have three loops around your hook.

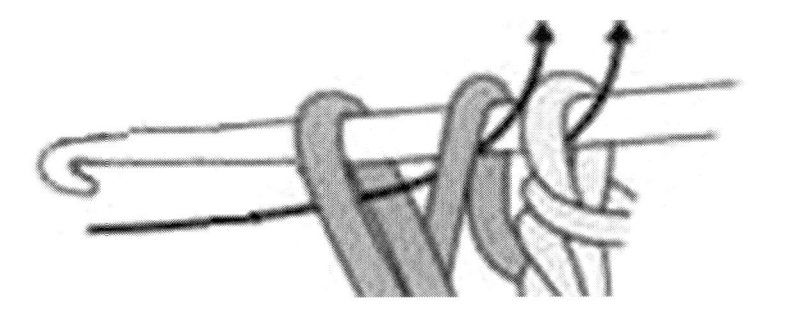

4. Yarn over, hook a thread, and slip it through the two loops around the hook. Do it twice.

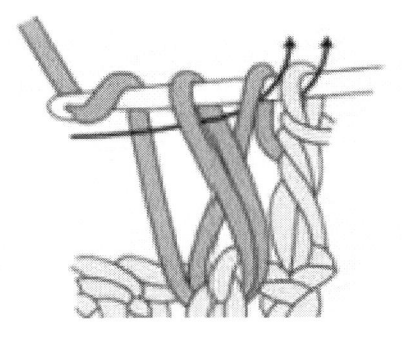

5. You can follow the same procedure for fpsc; you only need to use single crochet instead of double crochet.

How to Work a Back Post

Again, we will use dc to create bpdc. When you want to create the opposite effect of the front post, you need to use back post stitches. You can start from where your double crochet lesson has left off.

1. You already have a row of finished dc stitches. Turn your work (don't forget to look at the reminders posted on Turning Chain) and continue with the next row. Use ch-2 as your turning chain because bpdc stitches are shorter than normal dc stitches.
2. Yarn over and slip your hook from the back going to the front of the next post (the same with the front post, only in reverse) and to the back again.

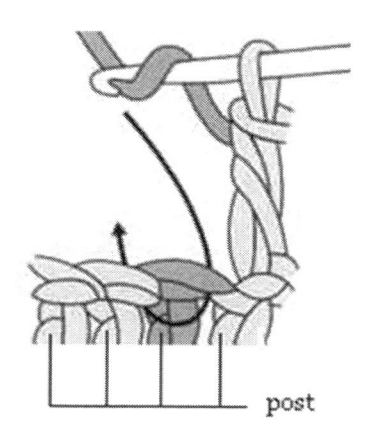

post

3. Hook a thread and guide it back to your initial position. You should produce three loops around your hook.

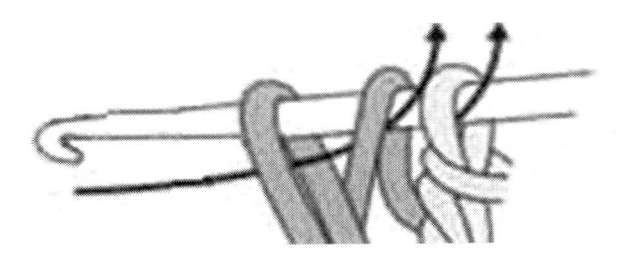

4. Yarn over, hook a thread, and slip it through the two loops around the hook. Do it twice.

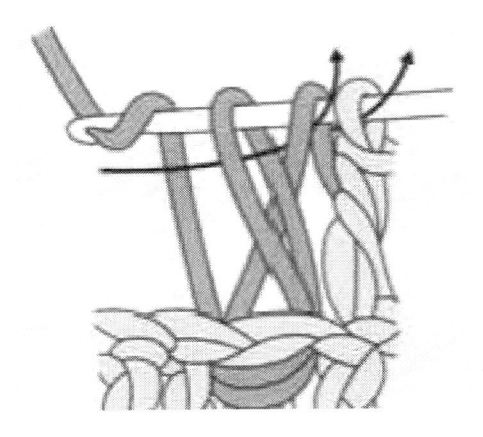

5. Follow the same procedure when working with bpsc; use single crochet instead of double crochet.

Chapter 4: Tunisian Crochet

Tunisian crochet is one of those crochets that requires a new set of tools aside from the one for regular crocheting. For instance, you must have a very long hook that would aid you in holding the loops. With the use of Tunisian crochet, you can combine it with common effects, crochet, and stitches. One major thing about the Tunisian stitches is that it has two passes—forward pass and reverse pass. In the forward pass, the stitches are picked into the hook while in the reverse pass, you work these stitches off the hook.

While there might still be a sort of confusion on how traditional crochet is different from Tunisian crochet, you must know that Tunisian crochet is an extension of traditional crochet. This means that Tunisian crochet is an advanced class for crochets who feel the need to improve their skills. This implies that there are a lot of differences between both of them. Some of these differences include:

Tools

In traditional crocheting, the hook used is just 6cm long. At the first end is a hook while the other is straight. The hook is made of either wood, plastic, or aluminum and it has a very user-friendly handle. However, in Tunisian crocheting, the hook is about 11cm to 14 cm long.

There is a knob usually attached to the end of the hook that helps prevent your stitches from falling. From the shaft to the handle, it has a very smooth surface, making it look like the needle used for knitting; however, this one has a hook head rather than a pointed mouth.

Construction

Having had a glimpse of the difference between the tools used in both crocheting types, we should know how stitches are constructed. You can only go a stitch at a time, i.e., you can only move to the next stitch after you have completed one. Once the row is completed, you make a series of chains and then start a new row with the same pattern.

This is different in the Tunisian crochet, as you have to begin with your foundational chain; afterward, work right to the left, drawing up your loops across the entire row. You'd use your hook to hold these loops. You'd notice you finish a loop before going to the next in traditional crocheting, but that's not the same in Tunisian crocheting as you work the loops across the row to the left side.

Fabrics

You might think of Tunisian crochet as weaving or knitting if you see the outcome of Tunisian crochet.

However, you can carry out a litmus test by making a swatch using both techniques, with the same yarn, hook and you'd see that there is an obvious difference between both of them. In traditional crochet, the fabric has a lot of stretch both horizontally and vertically. However, in Tunisian crochet, there are no stretches horizontally but a lot of stretches vertically.

Also, the edges in Tunisian crochet are even smoother and neater than those of traditional crochet. While their differences are clear, it is not to show which is better but to show how both can work together.

Getting Started

Once you get the basics of Tunisian crochet-like every other craft there is, you get to see how easy it can be. The truth about it is that you would always get better if you practice more. There are three basic stitches in Tunisian crochet that include simple stitches, knit stitches, and purl stitches.

The same way you cannot build a good house without a solid foundation is the same way you cannot execute a Tunisian crochet project without a foundation row and that is where we would begin.

The characteristic of the Tunisian crochet is that the picture on the front and back is clearly different. In addition, the mice can hardly stretch. Unlike "normal" crocheting, here, you have all the hands of a row on the needle. These are summarized in a first step and then mended in a second step. The needle is held like a knitting needle. Choose a crochet hook that is long and has a uniformly thick shaft. You can crochet Tunisian with wool and synthetic yarns.

Step 1: The basis is an air chain, which has to be crocheted loosely. The loops should be taken, as shown in the picture. You always start at the right edge of the crochet work.

Step 2: In the next step, knit the loop on the left edge with an envelope. After that, two slings are always embarrassed. When the last two loops are cut off, the first row is finished. Many styles of Tunisian crocheting arise with such two steps: grasping and chopping.

Step 3: For the subsequent rows, grasp the loops, as shown in the figure below from the vertical mesh wires. The stitching of these loops takes place as described in step 2.

Step 4: When you finish the work, the loops of the last row must be chained off. To do this, crochet a warp stitch in the vertical wire of each machine.

The Foundational Row and the Forward Pass

Here, you make as many stitches of chain and slip knot as you like using the yarn and hook. Afterward, turn the chain to have a good view of the back stitches rather than work on the frontal loop of the chain.

Once the back bump is visible, put your hook under the back stitches of the 2nd chain counting from the hook, then you twist the yarn to pull a loop up. Follow the same process till the last chain.

1. Turn the chain to see the back bump.

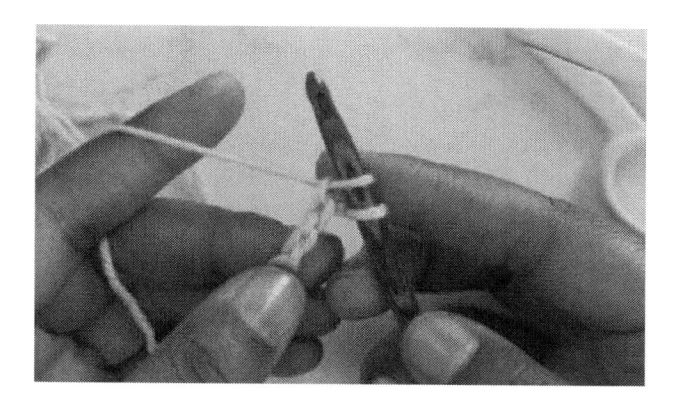

2. Put the hook into the bump on the back of the 2nd chain counting from where the hook is. Pull a loop up.

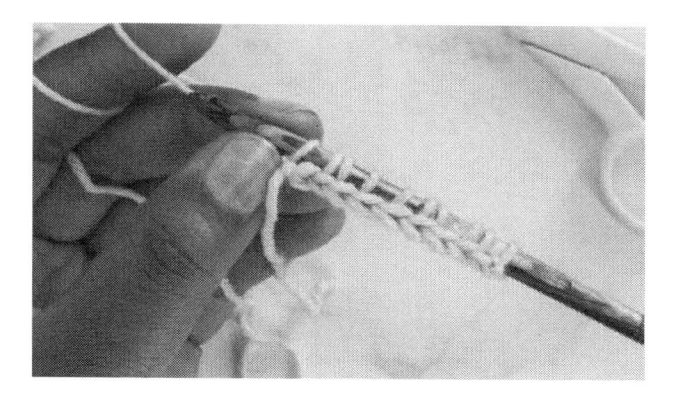

3. Follow the process until the loops are equivalent to the chains.

The big deal about the Tunisian crochet is the forward and reverse pass. After the forward pass, you have the reverse pass. Do you remember we have our loops on the hooks in the forward pass? Now, the reverse pass is simply taking these loops off the hook.

Your first chain, which involves that you yarn it and pull through the 1st loop on the hook, should always be the starting point for your reverse pass. This is so that you can maintain the project's hand. Afterward, pull the loops out of the hook by yarning and pulling it through the following two loops on the hook. Repeat this till you have just a loop on the hook.

1. First chain: yarn and pull through the 1st loop on the hook.

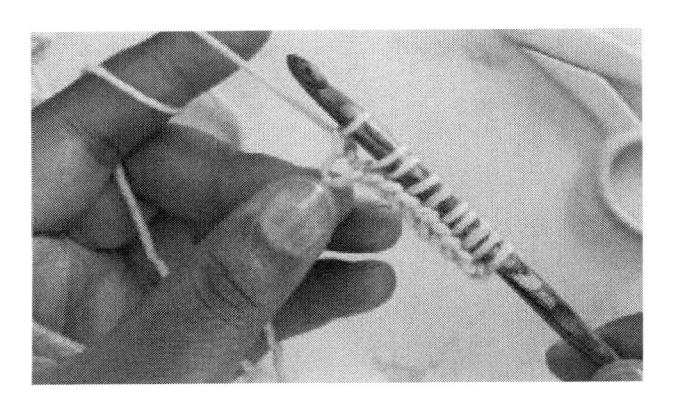

2. Yarn and pull through the following two loops on the hook.

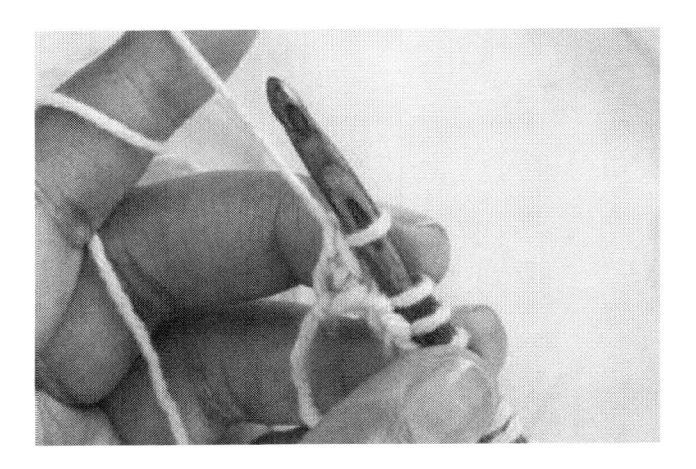

3. Repeat this till you have just a loop on the hook.

4. After we must have set the ball rolling with the foundation row, we move to the next which is the knit stitches.

Knit Stitches and the Forward Pass

The knit stitch begins by you identifying the stitch that you would be working into. You'd recall there is an outstanding loop on the hook, yeah? Now, this loop is what you'd use to begin the first stitch. This time, rather than starting with the stitch on the right, locate the second stitch and put your hook in between its two vertical bars.

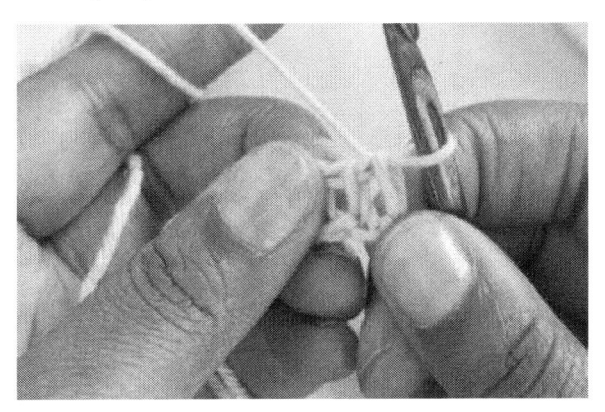

1. Put the hook in between the two vertical bars of the 2nd stitch.

2. Yarn and pull out a loop.

3. Follow through the process till the end of the row and stop with just a stitch left.

The final stitch here is quite tricky as you could get it all rough if you are not careful. To ensure it is neat, hold the project at the end with your forefinger and thumb, and then roll the stitch in between both fingers. Put the hook inside the two loops of the final stitch. Yarn and pull out a loop to finish the stitch.

Knit Stitches and the Reverse Pass

Follow through the reverse pass of the knit stitch the same way we did it in the foundation row. Start with the first chain, yarn, and pull two loops. Repeat it till one loop remains on the hook. The forward and reverse pass of the knit stitch can be continued to whatever length you desire.

Finishing or Binding

The essence of binding is to secure your stitches and to leave a neat edge. To achieve this, put your hook in between the vertical bars of the preceding stitch like you've done. This time, you don't continue but rather yarn and pull a loop. Afterward, pull through the loop that is on the hook, completing the slip stitch and securing the stitch.

Do this for the whole row. In the end, leave a long tail of the yarn then cut it off. Weave the tail in and out of the project.

Having learned this, we can now proceed to learn other stitches and some other projects.

Basic Tunisian Crochet Stitches

The Tunisian crochet has a lot of stitches, more than you can imagine. However, there are some basic stitches you should be familiar with before you can go advanced. Tunisian basic stitches can look almost alike to a novice, but in reality, there are slight variations between them, and that is where to insert your hook. That is, what makes these stitches different is where and how the hook is inserted.

Using the traditional crochet as an example, you'd recall that we insert our hook through the loop; however, in Tunisian crochet, we work our hook through the bars. Some Tunisian crochet stitches are worked through the horizontal bars; although, most of them are through the vertical. Since we have used the knit stitch to explain our foundation row and binding, there would be no need to discuss it in detail again.

The Simple Tunisian Stitch

Trust me when I say that the Simple Tunisian stitch is not like the knitting or other crochet stitches you'd have come across. It is the easiest Tunisian crochet stitch. Imagine the irony. It is called simple stitch because it is the first stitch a beginner must know in Tunisian crochet. It is best used for projects like cowls, headbands, etc., as it is good for making thick fabrics that provide a lot of warmth. The firmness of the fabric is dependent on the hook and yarn you use.

This stitch is very easy and straight to the point, and as such, it gives a lot of room for the experimentation of textures and colors. The Simple Tunisian stitch is done by:

1. Put the hook into the vertical bar of the next stitch from right to left.

2. Yarn and pull a loop.

3. Leave a loop on the hook and repeat the process until the end of the row. After you are done with the forward pass, do the reverse pass as explained.

Tunisian Reverse Stitch

This is much like the Simple Tunisian stitch just that it is in the reverse like the name suggests. Here, rather than work from the front, it is done from the back. You might have to have perfected the Simple Tunisian stitch to get this right. There is this ridge that the Tunisian Reverse Stitch adds to your work. It's best if you want to spice the texture of your work and also if you want to add different colors. The reverse stitch is done by:

1. Put the hook into the vertical bar from the back of the next stitch from the right side to the left side.

2. Yarn and pull a loop.

3. Leave a loop on the hook and carry out the process to the end of the row. Afterward, do the reverse pass.

Tunisian Knit Stitch

You'd recall that the Tunisian crochet is a mix of knitting and crocheting and yes, there is a Tunisian stitch that is called the Tunisian Knit Stitch that will make your project look like it was purely knitted.

Here, the front of the project where you use the Tunisian Knit stitch is very similar to the stockinet stitch while knitting, but when you turn it to the back, you'd see the difference between knitting and Tunisian crochet. You can use this stitch to make anything, be it accessories or garments, etc.

Tunisian Purl Stitch

The Tunisian Purl Stitch looks a lot like the Tunisian Reverse Stitch if you use color. However, you'd be able to spot the difference if you use multiple colors. This means you'd enjoy the outcome of your project better if you make use of multiple colors.

The Tunisian Purl Stitch is a little difficult than the other stitches listed above because of how much swinging it would take to put your hook in and out of the stitches. Once perfected, you can make a genius. The Tunisian Purl Stitch is done by:

1. Bringing the yarn to the front, put in the hook from the right side to the left side at the back of the frontal vertical bar of the next stitch.

2. Yarn and pull the loop.

3. Leave a loop on the hook and repeat the process to the end of the row. Afterward, do the reverse pass.

Tunisian Full Stitch

Tunisian full stitched projects are usually very fluffy and attract the hands to it a lot. I would advise you don't use white yarns so as not to get it easily dirty due to the number of touches it would get.

This stitch is more woven than the other stitches and has the texture at the front different from that at the back. You can use it to make scarves and other objects that are reversible.

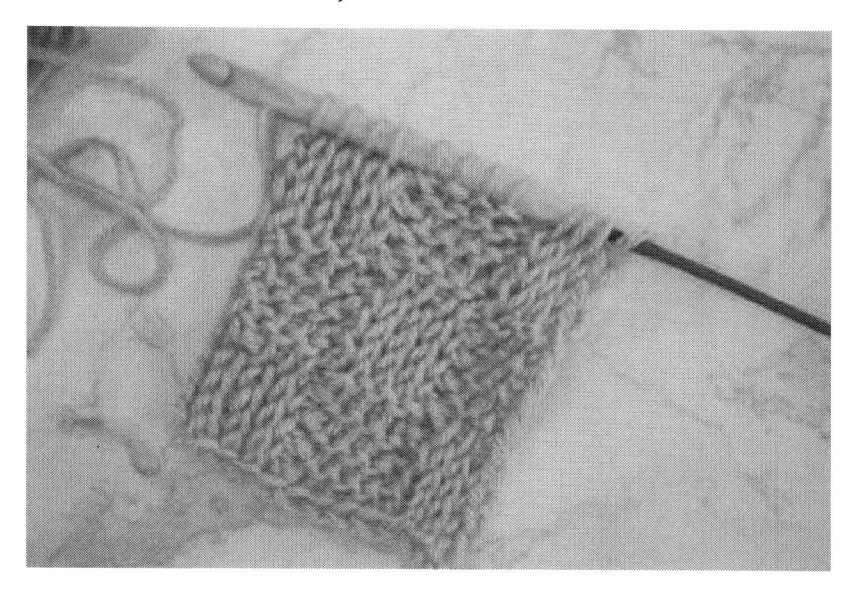

Chapter 5: Animal Crochet

Butterfly

Materials

- Crochet hook of size 3.5mm
- Yarn of category 4 worsted weight overcast, white or lavender color for the main body
- For wings Caron Cotton Cakes of Gerber Daisy color
- Safety eyes of size 9 mm and 10 mm
- Crochet thread of black color that will be used for eyebrows and lips
- Stuffing
- Tapestry needle

There are no variations in color throughout this design, although in the center for each wing there will be 2 rows (rows 13 and 14), which would be the main body color, instead of the color of the wing. Therefore, whenever you begin a new color over the next row, it is best to insert the hook into the stitching over the last stitch of Color A and pull up a loop, now, with Color B, yarn over and finish the stitching by drawing through loops with Color B. Remove your operating yarn in Color A and proceed to ch 1, then begin a new row with Color B. You'll also need to lower your yarn on opposite ends based on which wing section you focus on. Thus, for instance, you'll drop the yarn on either side during the first wing panel (pay attention to where your beginning yarn tail is; that will help you manage track!)

If you're operating on the second wing panel, you'll drop your thread from the first side on the opposing side; doing so will guarantee that somehow the edges are all pointing inward as you align the panels afterward to connect them.

Instructions

Body (make 2 panels) with 3.5mm hook

Perform the panels from the bottom up. Make one chain and turn at the edge of each row. All body panels are completed in a single color.

Row 1: Make four chains, single crochet across (3 stitches).

Row 2: Increase i.e., work two single crochet in the same stitch, work 1 single crochet, increase i.e., work two single crochet in the same stitch (5 stitches).

Row 3: Increase i.e., work two single crochet in the same stitch, work 3 single crochet, increase i.e., work two single crochet in the same stitch (7 stitches).

Row 4: Increase i.e., work two single crochet in the same stitch, work 5 single crochet, increase i.e., work two single crochet in the same stitch (9 stitches).

Rows 5–8: Single crochet across (9 stitches).

Row 9: Decrease i.e., work a regular single crochet, work 5 single crochet, decrease i.e. work a regular single crochet (7 stitches).

Rows 10–11: Single crochet across (7 stitches).

Row 12: Decrease i.e., work a regular single crochet, work 3 single crochet, decrease i.e., work a regular single crochet (5 stitches).

Rows 13–14: Single crochet across (5 stitches).

Now we will start the head.

Row 15: Ch 3, single crochet 2 along chs, then continue across row, single crochet 5 (7 stitches).

Row 16: Ch 3, Increase i.e., work two single crochet in the same stitch twice across chs, then continue across row, single crochet 5, increase i.e., work two single crochet in the same stitch twice (13 stitches).

Row 17: Increase i.e., work two single crochet in the same stitch, single crochet 11, increase i.e., work two single crochet in the same stitch (15 stitches).

Row 18: Increase i.e., work two single crochet in the same stitch, single crochet 13, increase i.e., work two single crochet in the same stitch (17 stitches).

Row 19: Increase i.e., work two single crochet in the same stitch, single crochet 15, increase i.e., work two single crochet in the same stitch (19 stitches).

Rows 20–23: Single crochet across (19 stitches).

Row 24: Decrease i.e., work a regular single crochet, single crochet 15, decrease i.e., work a regular single crochet (17 stitches).

Row 25: Decrease i.e., work a regular single crochet, single crochet 13, decrease i.e., work a regular single crochet (15 stitches).

Row 26: Single crochet across (15 stitches).

Row 27: Decrease i.e., work a regular single crochet, single crochet 11, decrease i.e., work a regular single crochet (13 stitches).

Row 28: Decrease i.e., work a regular single crochet, single crochet, work two half double crochet, work 3 double crochet, work 2 half double crochet 2, single crochet, decrease i.e., work a regular single crochet (11 stitches).

Tie off. Repeat for the second panel. Set panels aside for assembly later.

Wings *(make 4 panels in twos as explained below) with 3.5mm in Gerber Daisy*

Make 4 panels with a 3.5 mm crochet with a hook.

Row 1: Ch 5, single crochet across (4 stitches).

Row 2: Increase i.e., work two single crochet in the same stitch twice, single crochet 1, Increase i.e., work two single crochet in the same stitch (7 stitches).

Row 3: Single crochet 5, increase i.e., work two single crochet in the same stitch twice (9 stitches).

Row 4: Increase i.e., work two single crochet in the same stitch, single crochet 7, increase i.e., work two single crochet in the same stitch (11 stitches).

Row 5: Single crochet across (11 stitches).

Row 6: Single crochet 10, increase i.e., work two single crochet in the same stitch (12 stitches).

Rows 7–10: Single crochet across (12 stitches).

Row 11: Decrease i.e., work a regular single crochet, single crochet 10 (11 stitches).

Row 12: Single crochet across (11 stitches).

Switch to main body color.

Row 13: Single crochet across (11 stitches).

Row 14: Decrease i.e., work a regular single crochet, single crochet 9 (10 stitches).

Switch back to wing color.

Row 15: Decrease i.e., work a regular single crochet twice, single crochet 6 (8 stitches).

Row 16: Single crochet 6, increase i.e., work two single crochet in the same stitch twice (10 stitches).

Row 17: Increase i.e., work two single crochet in the same stitch twice, single crochet 6, decrease i.e., work a regular single crochet (11 stitches).

Rows 18–19: Single crochet across (11 stitches).

Row 20: Single crochet 10, increase i.e., work two single crochet in the same stitch (12 stitches).

Row 21: Single crochet 10, decrease i.e., work a regular single crochet (11 stitches).

Row 22: Single crochet across (11 stitches).

Row 23: Increase i.e., work two single crochet in the same stitch, single crochet 8, decrease i.e., work a regular single crochet (11 stitches).

Row 24: Decrease i.e., work a regular single crochet, single crochet 9 (10 stitches).

Row 25: Single crochet 8, decrease i.e., work a regular single crochet (9 stitches).

Row 26: Decrease i.e., work a regular single crochet, single crochet 7 (8 stitches).

Row 27: Single crochet 6, decrease i.e., work a regular single crochet (7 stitches).

Row 28: Decrease i.e., work a regular single crochet, single crochet 5 (6 stitches).

Tie off. For the second panel reiterate rows 1–28. Position all panels together, align both sides and start connecting the panels together through chaining 1 and sc in your main body color across the edges of the panel.

(Sc, ch 2, sc) at the top corner as well as the bottom wing arc, as shown in the picture below. Stuff approximately two-thirds of the manner across when you've crocheted. (The pictures below demonstrate two opposing wings (left and right); afterward, I noticed this could be confused!)

Try to ensure you are facing the front of the wing as you stitch across! On the other wing, here you will have to crochet throughout the direction opposite so the crochet edge faces out on both. Once the wings were completed, I intended to stitching the panel together just to provide the wings more depth by sewing around the two rows of that same main body color.

Antenna

We will create two antennas with a hook size of 3.5 mm and a color similar to the main body.

Row 1: Ch 7, single crochet across chs (6 stitches), ch 1, then, in the last stitch, crochet a cluster stitch.

Tie off. Weave in the ends.

Assembly

Step 1: Face and Feet

The very first step we have to do on the front panel would be to incorporate our facial characteristics.

First, incorporate safety eyes or you can use crochet thread of black color to knit pleasant eyes.

Use black crochet yarn to stitch onto the mouth.

Stitch on goosebumps and eyebrows if you like.

Step 2: Body and Wings

Now it's time to attach things together. Till now you will be having the following parts as shown in the picture below:

Cut about 30cm/15" long, 4 lengths of your main body yarn then put them aside for later. Position the 2 body panels, fitting both sides aligned. Ensure your butterfly's front faces you as you crochet outwards. Getting started from the left side of the head, start connecting the panels together through chaining one and only crocheting into your main color around the outside of the panels. Hold back it when you get to the lower part of your head. Take a long loop up, but for now, leave it.

From your tapestry needle as well as the length of yarn you put aside previously, position the first wing here between panels and knit via all three panels, the rear panel, the wing, and the front panel.

I have labeled that in the figure below to give you some idea of where you're going to stitch your pieces. Therefore, the "A" on the first wing matches the "A" on the body and even in that stitch down until about the "B" on the wing matches the "B" on the body. Whenever the wing is stitched between all the panels, tie a knot throughout the tails of the yarn to protect them and conceal them between panels of the body.

Keep crocheting down both sides of your face and head. Once you get to the wing, just crochet in the front panel stitches because this part has already been stitched closed. Hold back it when you go to the bottom of it. Take a long loop and end up leaving it for now.

With just the length of that same yarn that you put aside previously, position the second wing here between panels and connect it in the same way that you did for the first one. Bind the yarn tails inside the body panels in the same knot to protect. Keep crocheting about. Then, once you get to the wing, just crochet at the front panel stitches. Halt and stuff the lower part of the body. Keep crocheting up the side of your face. Stuff as you're going. Next, with that of the length of yarn which you set aside earlier, position the first antenna between panels and knit throughout all three panels, the rear panel, the antenna, and the front panel. Wrap the yarn tails around the inside of the body panels in the same knot to preserve. Proceed crocheting around the top of your head. Stuff as you're going. Position the second antenna the very same way that you did the first antenna. Keep crocheting around your head, topping up the stuffing as you need it. Close the slip stitch to the first stitch and wrap that off. Put the fabric tails back inside the piece.

And now the butterfly is ready.

Bumblebee

Materials

- Crochet hook of 4 mm
- Scissors
- Darning Needle
- Polyfill for stuffing
- Two safety eyes of size 12 mm

Instructions

Body

Starting with pink color.

Rnd 1: Make 6 single crochet into Magic Ring (6).

Rnd 2: Make two single crochet stitches in the same stitch around (12).

Rnd 3: Single crochet, make two single crochet stitches in the same stitch around (18).

Rnd 4: Single crochet 2, make two single crochet stitches in the same stitch around (24).

Rnd 5: Single crochet 3, make two single crochet stitches in the same stitch around (30).

Now switch your color from pink to black.

Rnd 6–8: Single crochet around (30).

Switch again to pink.

Rnd 9–11: Single crochet around (30).

Switch back to Black.

Rnd 12–14: Single crochet around (30).

Now again switch from black to pink.

Rnd 15: Single crochet around (30).

Rnd 16: Single crochet 3, crochet two stitches together using the invisible decrease method around (24).

Remember to add your safety eye to your project unless you miss your chance and mess it up!

Rnd 17: Single crochet 2, crochet two stitches together using the invisible decrease method around (18).

Rnd 18: Single crochet, crochet two stitches together using the invisible decrease method around (12).

Wings (make 2)

Rnd 1: 6 Single crochet into Magic Ring (6).

Rnd 2: make two single crochet stitches in the same stitch around (12).

Rnd 3–4: Single crochet around (12).

Finish off and leave tail for sewing.

Assembly

Now that you've got all of the pieces for your design, all you have to do is tie them up on both wings and you're done!

Seamus Shamrock

Materials

- Cotton worsted weight yarn
- Lightweight yarn for cheeks in pink color
- Black crochet thread for mouth
- Crochet hook of 3.5mm
- Tapestry needle
- Stuffing
- 8mm safety eyes

Instructions

Rnd 1: Magic ring with 9 single crochet (9 stitches).

Rnd 2: [Single crochet 2, work 2 single crochet into the same stitch]. Repeat [ ] around (12 stitches).

Rnd 3: [Single crochet 2, work 2 single crochet into the same stitch]. Repeat [ ] around (16 stitches).

Slip stitch to next stitch and tie off the first tip. Repeat rnds 1–3 for the second tip. Do not tie off the second tip. Continue to rnd 4 below after completing rnd 3 of the second tip.

Rnd 4: Join the tips by single crochet 16 around the tip on your hook and then ongoing to single crochet 16 around the first tip you made. (32 stitches) Slip stitch to beginning stitch.

Rnd 5: [Single crochet 7, work 2 single crochet into the same stitch]. Repeat [ ] around (36 stitches).

Rnd 6: [Single crochet 8, Work 2 single crochet into the same stitch]. Repeat [ ] around (40 stitches).

Rnd 7: [Single crochet 8, Work 2 single crochet stitch together]. Repeat [ ] around (36 stitches).

Rnd 8: [Single crochet 7, Work 2 single crochet stitch together]. Repeat [ ] around (32 stitches).

Rnd 9: [Single crochet 6, Work 2 single crochet stitch together]. Repeat [ ] around (28 stitches).

Rnd 10: Single crochet around (28 stitches).

Rnd 11: [Single crochet 5, Work 2 single crochet stitch together]. Repeat [ ] around (24 stitches).

Rnd 12: [Single crochet 4, Work 2 single crochet stitch together]. Repeat [ ] around (20 stitches).

Slip stitch to next stitch and tie off. Reiterate rounds 1 to 12 3 more times to make 4 leaves. Should not tie after the fourth leaf, then proceed down to rnd 13.

Rnd 13: Single crochet 7 on the fourth leaf on your hook. Join the next leaf by flattening the leaf and single crochet around the front half of the leaf (10 single crochet), join the next two leaves by single crochet 10 on each, then single crochet 3 of the first leaf (40 stitches total).

Rnd 14: [Single crochet 6, work 2 single crochet stitch together]. Repeat [ ] around (35 stitches).

Rnd 15: [Single crochet 3, work 2 single crochet stitch together]. Repeat [ ] around (28 stitches).

Rnd 16: [Single crochet 2, work 2 single crochet stitch together]. Repeat [ ] around (21 stitches).

Rnd 17: [Single crochet, work 2 single crochet stitch together]. Repeat [ ] around (14 stitches).

Rnd 18: Work 2 single crochet stitch together around (7 stitches).

Tie off, leaving a tail for closing. Weave tail through the front loops of each stitch, then down through the opening and out the back of Seamus. Tug gently on the tail to close. Place safety eyes, mouth, and cheeks.

Stem

Rnd 1: Magic ring 5 single crochet (5 stitches).

Rnd 2: Work 2 single crochet into the same stitch around (10 stitches).

Rnds 3–5: Single crochet around (10 stitches).

Stuff. Continue stuffing a little after each round.

Rnd 6: [Single crochet 3, Work 2 single crochet stitch together]. Repeat [ ] around (8 stitches).

Rnds 7–8: Single crochet around (8 stitches).

Rnd 9: [Single crochet 2, Work 2 single crochet stitch together]. Repeat [ ] around (6 stitches).

Rnds 10–15: Single crochet around (6 stitches).

Slip stitch to next stitching and tie off, allowing the tail being used to knit. Stitch the stem in between 2 leaves. If you're using a medium or fine Seamus weight yarn and a 2.25 mm crochet hook, it's going to get even lighter and will make a perfect keychain! Insert a loop to the top of Seamus and attach the keychain ring to make a cute sweet case, or simply fasten the jump circle through one of the stitching.

Chapter 6: Advanced Patterns and Projects

Super Scarf Crochet Pattern

Materials

- 6 skeins of super bulky Red Heart Stellar Yarn, weight #6 (24oz/ 480 yds total)
- 10.5 mm K-crochet hook
- Scissors
- Yarn needle

Gauge: 5 inches = 3 rows, 3 block stitches Flat measurement—123" L x 11" W

Notes

The pattern for this crochet scarf is going to be worked back and forth, flat, in rows from top to bottom. The turning chain is going to count as a stitch. We work row 2 into the stitches of the row before. All dcs are going to be worked in the gaps formed by the chains except for the final dc in row three—it shouldn't be in the chain links.

Instructions

Ch 3.

Row 1: Starting in the 3rd, dc all across beginning with the third chain from your hook—30 dc.

Row 2: Ch 1, turn, sc similar to turning chain, [ch 3, jump 4 dcs from the row before sc in the space that follows in between the dcs of the row before] rework six times, ch 3, sc in the final st—total 7 spaces of chain 3, 9 sc.

Row 3: Ch 3, turn, 4 dc in all spaces of chain-3 across, dc into the final st—30 dc.

Row 4: ch 1, turn, sc similar to turning chain, [ch 3, jump 4 dcs in the space that follows (between the st)] rework six times all across, ch 3, sc in the final st—total 7 spaces of chain 3, 9 sc.

Rows 5 to 146: Rework rows three and four.

Row 147: Rework row three.

Row 148: Dc in all stitches across—30 dc.

Finish off then weave in the ends.

Easy Textured Scarf

Materials

- 1 skein super bulky Caron Tea Cake (category six yarn) in Winterberry 11.5 mm P hook Scissors
- Yarn needle

Hdc blo—half double crochet back loop only where you insert your crochet hook only in the loop at the back instead of sliding your hook through the 2 top loops.

Completed size: Width: 8"

Before you sew: approximately 68" in length. After you sew together the ends: 33" in length.

Instructions

Ch 19.

Row 1: hdc in the second chain from your hook and all-around (18 hdc).

Row 2 to 62: chain 1, turn, in all stitches across hdc blo (18 hdc blo).

Finish off, leaving a long tail to sew.

Bring together both tails of your scarf. Whipstitch them together using the long end and the yarn needle.

Weave in all the ends.

Easy Crochet Coffee Cozy

Materials

- Scrap yarn
- Crochet hook 6mm
- Button
- Needle and thread
- Scissors

Instructions : Chain 10.

Row 1: Single-chain into the second chain from hook and into each following chain and turn. You should have 9 single crochets.

Row 2: Chain 1, single crochet into the first single crochet. Continue to single crochet into the one below. Turn. Repeat row 2 until your piece measures about 8 ¾". To make sure that this is the right size, measure against your favorite mug. The piece should cover the mug completely with a slight overlap. If you are a Starbucks fiend, this length will be sufficient.

Buttonhole

Slip stitch into the first four single crochets; make 6 chains; skip fifth single crochet and slip stitch into the last four single crochets. This loop will be big enough for a 25–28mm button. To accommodate a smaller button, reduce the number of chains when making the loop.

Border

Make 2 single crochets in the corner stitch, single crochet all along the edge until you reach the next corner. Make 2 single crochets in the corner stitch and then single crochet along the short edge. Make 1 single crochet in the bottom corner and continue until you reach the final corner. Single crochet once in the corner and in the first 3 slip stitches; slip stitch in the 4th single crochet; slip stitch in each of the chains where you have the button loop; single stitch in the next slip stitch and then single crochet in the last 3 stitches. Join the yarn and weave in the ends. Wrap your coffee cozy around a mug to check where the button needs to be and sew it in place.

Rope/Clothesline Easy Crochet Basket

Materials

- Crochet hook size Q
- 200ft of rope or clothesline

Instructions

Begin by creating a magic circle.

Step 1: sc 7 times within the magic circle.

Complete round by making an sl st on the first sc.

Step 2: Ch 2, sc twice in every stitch all across.

Complete round with an sl st.

Step 3: Ch 2, sc twice in first st, sc 1; rework.

Complete round with an sl st.

Step 4: Ch 2, sc twice in first st, sc 2; rework.

Complete round with an sl st.

Step 5: Ch 2, sc twice in first st, sc 3; rework.

Complete round with an sl st (don't ch 2).

Sc in every st all across continuing until the basket reaches your desired height.

If desired, flip your basket to have the right side out.

Sl st twice then fasten off.

Weave in the ends.

Market Bag

Materials

- Cotton yarn—it's perfect for this pattern as it's easy to wash and very sturdy.
- Crochet hook

Pro tip: To modify the length of the handles, chain your preferred distance in step 19 instead of chaining 50.

Instructions

Step 1: create a magic ring, chain 5 (counts as 1 treble crochet + 1 chain), **1 tr on the magic ring, chain 1; redo ten times from *,** join using a slip stitch on the fourth chain—12 tr + 12 ch 1 the gaps.

Step 2: Slip stitch into the first chain space, chain 5 (counts as 1 treble crochet + 1 chain), 1 tr on the same chain space, chain 1, **1 tr on the ch space that follows, chain 1, 1 treble crochet on same chain space, chain 1; redo from *** all through, join by making a slip stitch on the fourth chain—24 treble crochet + 24 chain-1 spaces.

Step 3: Slip stitch into the first chain space, chain 5 (counts as 1 treble crochet + 1 chain), 1 tr in the chain space that follows, ch 1, 1 tr on the same chain space, chain 1, **[1 tr in the chain space that follows, ch 1] two times, 1 tr on the same chain space, chain 1; repeat all through from *,** join by making a slip stitch on the fourth chain—36 treble crochet + 26 chain-1 spaces.

Step 4: Slip stitch into the first chain space, chain 5 (counts as 1 treble crochet + 1 chain), [1 tr in the chain space that follows, ch 1] two times, 1 tr on the same chain space, chain 1, **[1 tr in the chain space that follows, ch 1] thrice, 1 tr on the exact chain space, chain 1 then repeat all round from *,** join by making a slip stitch on the fourth chain—48 treble crochet + 48 chain-1 spaces.

Step 5: Slip stitch into the first chain space, chain 5 (counts as 1 treble crochet + 1 chain), [1 tr in the chain space that follows, ch 1] thrice, 1 tr on the same chain space, chain 1, **[1 tr in the chain space that follows, chain 1] four times, 1 tr on the exact chain space,**

chain 1, then repeat all round from *, join by making a slip stitch on the fourth chain—60 treble crochet + 60 chain-1 spaces.

Steps 6 to 16: Slip stitch into the first chain space, chain 5 (counts as 1 treble crochet + 1 chain), **1 tr in the chain space that follows, chain 1 then repeat all round from ***, join by making a slip stitch on the fourth chain—60 treble crochet + 60 chain-1 spaces.

Step 17: Chain 1 (counts as 1 single crochet), 1 sc in the chain space that follows, **1 sc in the stitch that follows, 1 sc in the chain space that follows; repeat all around from ***, join by making a slip stitch to chain 1—120 sc.

Step 18: chain 1 (counts as 1 single crochet), 1 sc in every stitch throughout the round, join to chain 1 using a slip stitch—120 sc.

Step 19: Chain 1 (counts as 1 single crochet), 1 sc in the 12 stitches that follow, chain 50, jump 31 stitches, 1 sc in all the 29 stitches that follow, chain 50, jump 31 stitches, 1 sc in all the 14 stitches that follow then join to chain 1 using a slip stitch—58 single crochet + 100 chains.

Step 20: Chain 1 (counts as 1 single crochet), 1 sc in the 14 stitches that follow, 1 sc in all the 50 chains that follow, 1 sc in all the 29 stitches that follow, 1 sc in all the 50 chains following, 1 sc in all the 14 stitches that follow, join to chain 1 using a slip stitch—158 sc.

Step 21: Chain 1 (counts as 1 single crochet), 1 sc in every stitch all through, invisible join to chain 1 then fasten off—158 single crochet.

Leg Warmers

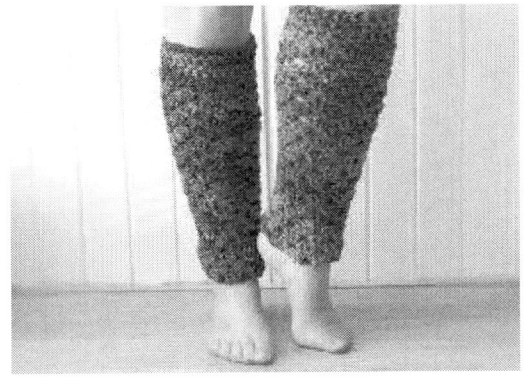

Materials

- 6 mm crochet hook
- 2–3 skeins
- Darning needle
- Scissors

Instructions

Ch 35.

Join with a slip stitch to the 1st chain. Ensure that your chain is not twisted.

Row 1: Chain 3 and double crochet into each chain, then join to the 3rd chain with a slip stitch.

Row 2–28: Chain 3 and double crochet into each stitch. Join the third chain with a slip stitch.

Bind off and weave in the ends.

Blanket Scarf

Materials

- 11.5 mm hook
- 318–424 yards of Bulky size 6 yarn

Gauge: 6 stitches x 4 rows = 4×4 square.

Length: 52 inches without the fringe.

Instructions

Row 1: Chain 28, then double crochet into the second chain until the last chain stitch, chain 2, then turn.

Row 2: Double crochet across, chain 2, and turn.

Repeat row 2 for 45 rows or until you achieve your desired length.

Finish off at the end of your last row and weave in the ends.

Crochet Face Scrubbies

Materials

- Yarn needle
- Crochet hook of 5mm
- Worsted weight cotton yarn

Instructions

Chain 4 and join with a slip stitch to create a ring.

Row 1: Chain 2, then single crochet into the center. (Chain 1 and single crochet into the center) Repeat 4 times. Chain 2 then join to the 1st stitch with a slip stitch; you should now have a total of 12 stitches around the circle.

Row 2: Chain 2 (half double crochet 2 times into the gap from the previous round, chain 1). Repeat 5 times. Half double crochet into the gap formed from the previous round. Ch 1 then join into the 1st stitch with a slip stitch; you should now have 18 stitches around the circle.

Row 3: Chain 2 (single crochet, chain 1). Repeat 8 times. Single crochet 2, then join to the 1st stitch with a slip stitch; 27 stitches around the circle.

Row 4: Chain 1 (chain 3 and slip stitch into the next stitch, sc). Repeat 12 times. Chain 3 then slip stitch in the final stitch.

Secure the final stitch, then weave in the ends with a yarn needle.

Dainty Baby Sweater

Materials

- 3-ply fingering/baby yarn
- Crochet hook of 5.5 mm/GE

Instructions

Back

Round 1: Make 49 ch, then dc in the 2nd loop from the hook, dc in each of the next 2 chains, and then turn to form 12 groups of 2 dcs.

Round 2: Make ch 4, sc in the first ch space across, and then work to the last sc of the previous row, chain 3, and turn.

Round 3: Make 2 dc in the first loop, make 1 ch, 3 dc in next ch, and then chain-loop across.

Round 4–23: Repeat rounds 1–3, 10 times.

Front

Round 1: Make ch 4, sc in the first ch space, then chain 3, sc in the next chain thrice, chain 3 again, 4 chains, loop thrice.

Round 2: Make a double chain in the first 3 chain loops. Make chain 1, 3 dc in the next loop thrice, and then turn.

Rounds 3–23: Repeat the first 2 rounds until they measure the same as the ones on the back and fasten off.

Collar and Facing

Round 1: Make 3 chains in the next space, and repeat the process around the entire fabric. Make sure to work on both front and back ends.

Round 2: In the first space, make 3 dc, then make 4 dc in the next ch space, then join, and turn.

Round 3: Make 3 chains in the next space, and repeat the process around the entire fabric. Make sure to work on both front and back ends.

Round 4: In the next space, make 3 dc, then make 4 dc in the next ch space, then join, and turn.

Round 5: Make another 3 chains in the next space, and repeat the process around the entire fabric. Make sure to work on both front and back ends.

Round 6: Repeat rounds 2 and 4 but make 160 stitches.

Round 7–8: Make chain 3 and then dc in the first ch space 48 times, ch 1 21 times, 3 dc in the next space, picot 27 times, dc 21 times, and then sl stitch to join.

Sleeves

Round 1: Chain 4 and then sc in the next space, ch 3 13 times, ch 3 again, and turn.

Round 2: Make 2 dc in the first chain, 3 dc loop, and turn.

Rounds 3–15: Repeat rows 1 and 2.

Round 16: Make 2 dc in the first 3-ch loop, picot, and then fasten off.

Finishing

Sew the sleeves on and then fasten off the seams. Sew a ribbon in the middle.

Quick Little Crochet Bag

Materials

- Red heart unforgettable yarn
- Crochet hook of 5.50 mm size I
- Safety pins or yarn pins
- Yarn needle

Size: 5-inch square.

Gauge: 16 rows x 16 sts = 4 inches in the pattern—though, the gauge isn't quite significant since the bag is not an item that's fitted.

Notes: From the second row henceforth, there won't be a starting chain. Simply go with the pattern, it's going to work out just fine.

Instructions

Base Piece

Row 1: Ch 19, sc in 2nd chain from your hook and all remaining chains across, 18 sc.

Row 2: Turn, sk 1 sc, (sc, dc) in the sc that follows, rework all across from *, 18 sts.

Rows 3 to 44: Turn, (sc, dc) in every sc all across, 18 sts.

Cut the yarn and then weave in the ends.

Fold and Join

Fold work so that its bottom (row forty-four) is laying over in between rows six and seven, leaving a flap of six rows outside the section that is folded. Hold it in place by adding a pin or 2 on either side.

Row 1: affix to one of the corners at the bottom of the bag that is folded, sc twenty times evenly along the length of bag in the section that's folded—don't sc on the sections of unfolded flaps, ch 150, sc twenty times evenly along the length of bag in the section that's folded—190 stitches.

Row 2: turn, chain 1, slip stitch in every stitch across the first row—190 stitches.

Cut the yarn then weave the loose ends.

Modern Taupe Crochet Belt

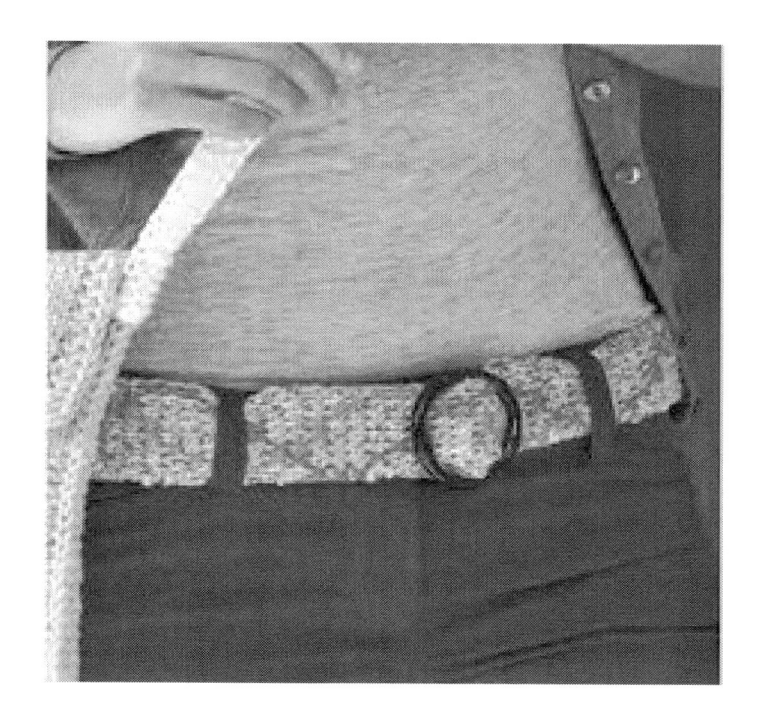

Materials

- 1 Skein Vanna's Choice Lion Brand (or preferred worsted weight yarn)
- Wood buttons
- Tapestry needle
- Crochet hook of 5.5 mm size I
- Tape measure
- Scissors

Instructions

Ch 14.

Row 1: Create one dc in the fifth chain from your hook, skip 2 chains then (dc, ch 1, dc) in the chain that follows, Rework all across to row's end from.

Row 2: Ch 4, turn. Create one dc in the 1st "V" (chain one space from the row before), create (dc, ch 1, dc) in every "V" (chain one space from the row before) all across.

Rework the second row until the belt reaches your preferred length. Weave in all the ends.

Creating the Belt Ties

Cut out six yarn pieces measuring 90" in length each.

Fold every piece of yarn in half, then in half once more.

Every end of the belt is going to have three strands attached to it.

While you hold one of the folded strands, find the tip with 2 loops (the other tips going to have 2 cut ends and 1 loop.

Position the end with 2 loops within one edge and then pull the other tip through.

Tighten by pulling gently then rework using the other 2 strands at the tip of your belt.

Rework using the remaining side of the belt.

String the wood beads to the tails of yarn using a tapestry needle. To prevent the beads from slipping off, tie a knot at the tips.

Crochet Flower Bracelet

Materials

- Crochet hook size E
- DMC cotton pearl size 5
- Scissors
- Cute button
- Yarn needle

Instructions

This pattern creates the bracelet by joining three flowers. Create the pattern below three times then use the exact thread you used for flowers to sew together. Gauge is not relevant.

Ch 4; join to the first chain using sl st to create a ring.

Round 1: Ch 1, sc eight times in ring; join to first sc using sl st—8 sc.

Round 2: Ch 1, sc in the exact stitch as join, chain 3; [sc in the following sc, chain 3] seven times; join to first sc using sl st—8 ch-3 spaces and 8 sc.

Round 3: Sl st in following chain 3 space, chain 3 (it's going to count as dc), dc two times in the same chain 3 space, chain 2; [dc three times in following chain 3 space, chain 2] seven times; join to top of starting chain using sl st—8 ch-2 spaces and 24 dc.

Round 4: Ch 2, dc 2 together, [chain 3, sc in following chain 2 space, chain 3, dc 3 together] seven times, chain 3, sc in following chain 2 space, attach to ch 1, hdc over top (dc 2 times together which is going to count as chain 3 space)—16 ch-3 spaces, 18 sc dc2tog, and 7 dc3tog.

Finishing

Sew together the flowers (two petals to two petals).

Sew the button on, then fasten to the flower in the opposite through the hole that's found in the flower motif naturally.

Hand Towels

Materials

- Ball(s) of knit pick cotlin yarn, depending on the colors you prefer. Use more colors to make a striped hand towel
- Crochet hook of 5.5 mm size H
- Tapestry needle
- Scissor
- Sewing needle and thread (optional)
- Button (optional)
- Yarn needle

Gauge: 14 rows and 12 stitches as 4 inches (10 cm) in the pattern.

Instructions

To make this crochet hand towel, you should know how to do a pique stitch. It is quite simple to work with—just yarn over (yo) and then insert the hook into the 3rd chain (ch-3) from the hook; you can also do this from the first stitch (st) of the row.

Yarn over and then draw a loop. Make 3 loops on the hook, and your stitch will look like a double crochet stitch (dc). Then yarn over and draw it through the 3 loops; in this way, you will have 2 loops on the hook.

Yarn over to insert the hook into the same chain, and draw up a loop; in this way, you will have 4 loops. It will be your first complete pique stitch.

Now, you will do these instructions for pique stitch to crochet a hand towel.

If you are thinking of making a striped hand towel, here's how you can lose a chain for a starting chain.

Row 1: Starting from the 3rd chain (ch-3), work a pique stitch in every 30 stitches (sts).

Row 2: Single crochet stitch (sc) in every stitch. Then work in chain 2 for a turning chain and turn.

Row 3: Now pique stitch in every stitch and then work chain 1 for a turning chain and turn.

Repeat row 2, row 3, and row 4 and then change to the new yarn, e.g., color 1.

Then repeat row 3 and row 2, 2 times and change to another color yarn, e.g., color 2.

Now, repeat row 3 and row 2, 1 time and then change to a different color yarn, e.g., color 3.

Repeat row 3 and row 2, 2 times, change to the color yarn 2, and then repeat row 3 and row 2 one time.

Change to a different color yarn, e.g., color 4, and repeat row 3 and row 2, 2 times.

Change to the color 2 yarn and then repeat row 3 and row 2, 7 times.

Change to the color 4 yarn and then repeat row 3 and row 2, 2 times.

Change to the color 2 yarn and then repeat row 3 and row 2, 1 time.

Change to the color 3 yarn and then repeat row 3 and row 2, 2 times.

Change to the color 2 yarn and then repeat row 3 and row 2, 1 time.

Change to the color 1 yarn and then repeat row 3 and row 2, 2 times.

Change to the color 2 yarn and then repeat row 3 and row 2, 3 times.

Now, you are done; secure the last stitch, trim the yarn and weave in all the ends.

Simple Crochet Wrap Bracelet

Materials

- DMC Pearl Cotton Embroidery Thread and Metallic Size 10 of Aunt Lydia's Crochet Cotton crochet (gold)
- Scissors
- Button
- Crochet hook of 2.75mm size C2

Instructions

Chain as enough chains as necessary for wrapping 3 times around your wrist; feel free to make more chains so that the bracelet wraps around the intended wrist as many times as desired.

Once you are done creating your preferred length of chain, create a big additional stitch—which is going to become the loop.

Create one more chain past the huge additional ch st (while working the final ch st, it's recommended to hold the big chain stitch).

Create sl st into the second chain from the hook (the one following the huge stitch).

Sl st across all chains then finish off.

Grab the ending tail and beginning tail to affix a button of your choice.

Secure the button by tying two square knots. Cut ends off, then secure further by applying glue.

Once you have wrapped the bracelet around the ankle or wrist as many ties as possible, use the loop to fasten the button.

Two Color Bracelet

Materials

- Crochet hook of 3mm size D
- 100% cotton yarn

Finished size: designed to fit any adult hand easily.

Colors used: color B and color A.

Gauge: not significant.

Instructions

Row 1: Ch 44 using color A, ss in 1st ch ensuring that the chain isn't twisted.

Chain one and single crochet in the 1st stitch, create one sc in all chains up to the end, ss.

If the bracelet you require is smaller or bigger, simply make the beginning ch smaller or bigger, just ensure that the number of chains is even.

Now is the perfect time to test whether the bracelet is going to fit and whether it's going to be comfy to put on.

Row 2: Attach color B. ch 1, sc in exact stitch, **ch 1, sk one stitch, 1 sc, repeat all across from ***, finish using ss.

Row 3: Affix color A in the chain one space in between 2 sc then repeat the second row.

Row 4: Ch 1, sc in exact stitch, sc in all stitches across, 1 ss. Clip yarn, then weave in the tips.

Striped Circle Coasters with a Scalloped Edge

Materials

- 4 weight yarn, 4 balls. 2 balls of color A, 2 balls of color B
- Crochet hook size H

Abbreviations Used

- Chain (Ch)
- Slip Stitch (Sl St)
- Single Crochet (Sc)
- Double Crochet (Dc)

Instructions

To Make the Bottom

Round 1: Starting at center with color A, Ch 4. 11 Dc in 4th Ch from hook. Sl St in top stitch of starting chain.

Round 2: Drop color A, attach color B, Ch 1, Sc in the same place as Sl St, *2 Sc in next stitch, Sc in next stitch. Repeat from * to * around. Join.

Round 3: Drop color B, pick up color A. Ch 3, Dc in each stitch around, increasing 12 Dc evenly around. To increase a Dc, make 2 Dc in 1 stitch.

Round 4: Drop color A, pick up color B, Ch 1. Sc in each stitch around, increasing 6 Sc evenly around.

Repeat rounds 3 and 4 alternately until the piece measures about ¼ inch larger all around the bottom of the glass, ending with round 3.

To Make the Edging

Round 1: Drop color A and pick up color B. Turn and make Sc in the back loop of each stitch around. Join.

Round 2: Drop color B, pick up color A. Sc in the same place as Sl St. *Ch 5, 3 Dc where last Sc was made, skip 3 Sc, Sc in next Sc. Repeat from * to * around. Join. Cut off color A.

Round 3: Pick up color B, *5 Sc in Ch 5 loop, Sc in next 3 Dc. Repeat from * to * around. Join and break off.

Attach color B and, working over free loops of the last Dc round of the Bottom, work a second edging as follows:

Round 1: Sc in each stitch around, increased by 8 Sc evenly around. Join.

Round 2: Same as round 2 of 1st edging, skipping 2 (instead of 3) stitches. Join and break off. Complete as for 1st edging.

Conclusion

There you have it, everything you need to know to get you started in the world of crochet, and beginning your patterns now! I know there is a lot of excitement when you are first starting this hobby, and it is hard to get discouraged when you are excited about something, but I want to warn you… you have to practice.

Your choice of crochet border can seriously make your piece of crochet a masterpiece or a boring piece of clothing. These amazing patterns are the perfect way to make your design complete and appealing to the eyes. Learn these gorgeous patterns to create perfect projects and brag about them to everyone around you. The art of crochet is one of the skills that has multiple benefits at once.

Learning to crochet is a skill you will find useful because you can take what you learn and turn it into garments and projects that provide joy and utility for people who use them. With your imagination, you can take your new knowledge of the stitches and create your patterns and designs to make a variety of projects of your own.

Keep your hands relaxed so that you are not tensing up and tiring your fingers and hands. By relaxing, your stitches will come freely, and by practicing, you will be able to unravel the stitches that don't measure up to your standard, retry the stitches over and over again.

You will find you like some stitches more than others. By mastering the basic stitches, you will be able to tolerate your least favorites.

Join the crochet community by putting your new skills into action. Relax and enjoy using what you learn to produce actual items that you can use and enjoy.

Be creative and artistic and heal your mind and soul from emotional stress. This craft has the power to free anyone from the heaviness of his reality and break out from his own thoughts. This skill is a practical talent that should be passed down from one generation to the next.

The discovery or invention of crochet can be considered as one of the best gifts for humanity as it can be a cure and a medicine to a wounded soul and it might as well boost the self-esteem of people who are struggling with low self-esteem and depression by giving them a sense of gratification and accomplishment while seeing what's being created by their own hands.

It is a lovely feeling to watch a masterpiece being created and to think that you made it! It's a satisfying feeling that can help to relieve stress, calm down, keep the mind busy, get rid of worries and troubles, and forget about the harsh reality. This is what we can consider mindfulness crochet, which is a magnificent way to approach crochet as a way to reduce stress and benefit the health of the mind and body. By learning these amazing edging patterns you will get countless benefits from lifting your mood to calming your mind while boosting the sense of creativity and the feeling of happiness.

Crocheting is an enjoyable hobby, and I hope you will always have the desire to crochet during your free time. The best way to make it easy for you to learn how to crochet is by making a good hook choice.

Take small breaks in between your crocheting and exercising, we also have some more tips that can help you to be careful while crocheting. Our hand posture plays a big role in crocheting.

Crocheting is a fun craft to try your hand at. The learning curve is not steep as it only takes a few tries to get the hang of crocheting. Once you start, you will find yourself eager and interested in taking on bigger and more challenging projects. However, even the advanced projects are quite easy to master once you know the basics, so always have fun and if you feel like you've hit a roadblock, don't worry, just look back on this book or the patterns, and you'll be on the right track in no time.

Printed in Great Britain
by Amazon